T0115006

PARENTUALITY

How to Have an Amazing Relationship with Your Child

Dr Linda Mallory

BALBOA.
PRESS
A DIVISION OF HAY HOUSE

Balboa Press books may be ordered through booksellers or by contacting:

Balboa Press
A Division of Hay House
1663 Liberty Drive
Bloomington, IN 47403
www.balboapress.com
1 (877) 407-4847

Images supplied by avtarbains.co.uk.

Printed in the United States of America.

ISBN: 978-1-4525-9496-5 (sc)
ISBN: 978-1-4525-9497-2 (e)

Library of Congress Control Number: 2014905597

Balboa Press rev. date: 4/14/2014

ACKNOWLEDGEMENTS

To Mrs Audsley, my primary school teacher, who inspired me to teach;

To all the children I have had the privilege to meet as a teacher and educational psychologist, for their insight and honesty;

To my family for providing the experiences that have taught me so much;

To Jennifer Manson for doing an amazing job of editing and shaping this book, for supporting me in the process of finding my flow as a writer and for her inspiration;

For Paul Manson and Jackie Charley for proofreading the book;

To Victoria Millar for reading the first draft and giving some valuable suggestions and insights;

To Lucy Whittington for helping me find my purpose;

Thank you.

DEDICATION

To Av, Fred and Tom, my soul mates
and greatest teachers.

*"Let us be grateful to people who make us
happy, they are the charming gardeners
who make our souls blossom."*
Marcel Proust

CONTENTS

INTRODUCTION

Thank you for picking up this book. I wish I could have read this book, or one like it, before meeting my first child, to give me then some of the insights I have now. There was so much I didn't know. So much I wish I had known.

That was my motivation to create the concept of The Why Parent, and to write this book.

Over the last few years, as an educational psychologist, and, more importantly, as a parent, I have analysed the mountains of material on parenting. Much of the information out there focuses on the "what" and the "how" of parenting. I wanted to delve deeper into the "why" of parenting.

This book is the result of that enquiry into the why; it is my gift to you as a parent on your heartfelt parenting journey.

This book is for you if you are reflecting on your parenting and want an amazing long-term relationship with your children; it is for you if you need to find your purpose and "why" as a parent.

This book is not about me as an educational psychologist and a parent coach giving you a quick "behaviour fix" of what to do with your child – it is to help you explore and find your own "why" of parenting. When I use parents in this book I am using an inclusive term to mean anyone who has a main caring relationship with their children. single parents, foster or adoptive parents, carers and guardians.

"Parentuality," is a word to describe the awakening we have as parents when we become caregivers. The experience of connecting on a conscious level with ourselves, our children, and life. Parentuality is a higher level of consciousness in our parenting, which helps us have an amazing relationship with our children.

If you are ready to embark on that journey, then let's get started ...

CHAPTER ONE

FIND YOUR "WHY" AS A PARENT

"*Nothing has a stronger influence psychologically on their environment and especially on their children than the unlived life of the parent.*"

Carl Jung

It feels like a dream when you hold your child for the first time and whisper, "hello." What follows is a journey of accelerated enlightenment, a warp speed *Star Trek* voyage into the unknown where you can "boldly go" or, as I did, "fumble awkwardly."

Holding my first child, I felt I was entering alien territory and I asked myself, "Am I going to mess this up?"

After nine years of parenting, of finding my way through the ecology of parent and child, this book is a journey of reflection.

In the hectic schedule of a busy day I am encouraging you to give yourself permission and time to stop and reflect on you, your parenting and your relationship with your child.

Explore the possibility of enjoying every single moment with your child, of following your own inner guidance; to "boldly go" with confidence in your own judgement.

Trust yourself

The main thing I would like to say if I bumped into my past, new-parent self would be: "Be present, enjoy the moment and really understand why you are doing what you are doing."

As parents we are bombarded with endless information from books, magazines, websites and TV programmes that make us feel guilty that we are not doing what we "could" be doing. We feel that we "should" be implementing the latest "evidence-based" behaviour technique with our children.

When we use those words of "could" and "should", that implies guilt or shame.

I would have loved to have discovered my "why" as a parent, back when I was heavily pregnant, watching the Athens Olympics and knitting a cot blanket. It is fascinating that I thought being pregnant meant that I "should" be knitting!

Having now arrived at a "pit stop" moment in my parenting journey (my children now are nine and eight), what I would like to say to parents is this:

> Every single moment can be cherished and enjoyed.

Even those moments that are frustrating and overwhelming are amazing learning opportunities for us and our children.

Allowing ourselves space to learn

Our children are our greatest teachers if we allow them to be. Even the tantrums in supermarkets and those moments when they refuse to eat the food we have spent hours lovingly preparing can be enjoyed if we let ourselves.

If we truly listen to our children they can show us who we really are and who they need to be.

When things go wrong, that feeling of being totally overwhelmed, thinking, "What can I do to make this situation better?" can be a learning opportunity. We can ask ourselves, "What is it about this situation that is making me react like this?" "Why is it that I am feeling frustrated?" "Why am I sounding like my mum?" and give ourselves the opportunity to change.

Usually it is not our children causing this reaction, it is our past experiences and our subconscious coming into play, triggering off these overwhelming feelings. It is okay to have these moments that are difficult and challenging. Ultimately our children are teaching us something about our reactions; they can give us so much in terms of learning about ourselves and learning how to connect with them so that we can give them what they need.

It is that reciprocity between our children teaching us and us being able to help them through difficult and challenging emotions and situations that makes parenting the amazing voyage of discovery it is. The biggest challenge of parenting is to embrace those moments of joy and frustration in equal measure, and to discover our "why" of parenting.

Connecting with ourselves; teaching our children

The parenting journey, as described in this book and following The Why Parent approach, takes us first inside ourselves, to discover and connect with us as individuals; and then out again, equipped with these insights and that deeper connection into our relationship with our children, to connect deeply with them, and to guide them to be the people they were born to be.

Being authentic with ourselves and our children

Once we start thinking of every single situation with our children as a learning opportunity, this helps us become more conscious about what we focus on, particularly our thoughts, feelings and emotions.

Our children display very big emotions that they are sometimes not quite sure how to express, for example the tantrum in the supermarket, the refusal to tidy up, not putting on a coat when it is cold. They have overwhelming emotions and feelings, which they are trying to process. It's our job to help them process those emotions – to feel that frustration, confusion or indeed happiness – and express them appropriately out into the world; and doing so helps us, too.

Once we stand back and remember not to take those moments personally, or as indicating failure in ourselves; we become more conscious about what we are thinking and saying to our children, we begin to develop a more authentic relationship with ourselves.

Sometimes we, too, can get overwhelmed by our feelings of anger or frustration and can feel guilty about what we are thinking as parents.

Parenting for me has become a process of becoming more conscious about my emotions and therefore being more honest and authentic with what I am thinking and feeling.

Our children as role models

Our children are brilliant role models, showing us how to be honest and open with our thoughts and feelings. We can acknowledge our feelings and let them grow. We can step into those emotions and become a role model for our children in turn, showing them how to experience emotions and really feel them. It is a practice we become better at the more we undertake it, just like meditation, yoga or focusing on a muscle group by lifting weights in the gym.

That process helps us to build an authentic relationship with ourselves, and ultimately an amazing relationship with our children.

Really feeling our emotions

When we give a name to our emotions and also really feel them, we become more comfortable with those feelings of frustration; we know ourselves better as parents. Some people think it is selfish focusing on our feelings, and that we should focus on our children's emotions; but in order to really empathise with our children and truly understand them, to really connect with our children when they feel frustrated or angry, we need to understand our own emotions, too.

My experience working with parents, myself included, is that we feel guilty or overwhelmed when we are angry or frustrated. We move quickly on to the next situation with the subconscious message to our children that there is no time to have emotions.

Once we start being more authentic with ourselves, then our children are free to be who they need to be. It is that reciprocal relationship and connection that is so important and makes us human. It is such a joy to have that space and time to connect.

I think sometimes we run around being so busy that we lose those moments of authentic connections. We are so distracted by our TV, computer screens and telephones. It is not always the amount of time that counts in a connection with our children. Sometimes five minutes of really listening can be more enlightening than an hour of being in the same room with all the family members being distracted.

Joy as well as frustration

As parents we also need to acknowledge those moments of joy and complete elation when our children demonstrate something amazing. Whether it is a drawing, learning to ride a bike for the first time or beginning to swim – what my eldest son Fred calls a "treasure of skills" – it is those moments that make us feel total joy as parents. We can learn from the way children celebrate the simple moments of life.

As parents we are often worried about what happened yesterday, anxious about what will be happening tomorrow, rather than just being present, enjoying the moment and really feeling the now with our children.

Calm, connected and conscious - three levels of mind

To go a little deeper into understanding how we make decisions as parents, I'll start with a very simplistic explanation of how the brain works. The brain is essentially made up of three main parts: the brain stem, limbic system and prefrontal cortex.

The brain stem controls our fight and flight responses, which activate when we come up against something threatening, such as being mugged or being shouted at randomly by someone in the street. The natural instinct for survival kicks in.

The middle section of our brain, the limbic system, is the emotional-response part of the brain. This area is where our personal narratives, memories and stories come into play. We link our emotions to previous situations such as a bad experience we had at school. A teacher may have shouted at us for something we did, and a subsequent incident, such as someone raising their voice, may remind us of that moment and instantaneously transport us back to that time.

We can revisit an experience as a result of smells or sights and certain associations we might have with that memory. In that moment we are connected with the limbic system or emotional part of the brain.

The prefrontal cortex is the front area of the brain. This is where reasoning occurs, and our higher executive functions and thinking skills are located. Ideally when we are talking to our children it is useful to activate this strategic part of the brain in ourselves, and our children so that we empower them to think of a solution, and also to solve similar problems they might encounter in the future.

I have found that when working with children and parents, or indeed trying to understand my responses to my own children, it is useful to have a three-level approach to reflect on where thoughts, emotions and beliefs are coming from.

I call this: "The Why Parent process". It focuses on a calm, connected, and conscious approach and relates to the three main areas of the brain.

Calm

Let us go back to thinking about a fight or flight response to a situation such as being shouted at. The first stage of the process is to focus on regaining a calm state.

How can we be totally calm about a feeling of threat? For example, how can we go from that self talk of, "My child is having a tantrum in the supermarket. I am frightened of being judged by other parents," to reframe it to, "My child is really frustrated about something. I need to find out why they are frustrated. How can I be calm so I can respond in a conscious way?"

If we mirror the tantrum and anxiety by worrying about other people's judgements we become fearful; the child will pick up that energy of fear and the tantrum will naturally escalate. When we stay calm and focus on our child's needs, not on judging the tantrum, anxious behaviour is more likely to de-escalate.

Connected

The second stage of The Why Parent process is to demonstrate a connected response. This corresponds to the middle section of the brain, finding an association, memory or story to link the limbic system part of the brain. A positive emotional response would be to ask ourselves is, "How can I really connect with my child?"

We might be more conscious of using eye contact, really getting down to their level; we might try to understand what they are experiencing, seeing, thinking and feeling in the moment. Our children are making a link and an associated story with that moment; that is part of developing memories.

How we connect to our children makes a huge contribution to how that memory is stored and what lessons are taken from it. Getting down to their level, giving them a hug and physical contact or reassuring words can help that connection – some children like physical contact; some children like verbal contact and need to be comforted verbally.

Asking the question, "What does my child need right now?" supports the connection with our children at a very challenging time for them emotionally.

Conscious

The third part of the process is being able to understand our reactions in relation to the prefrontal cortex, the reasoning and decision-making part of the brain. We need to ask ourselves, "What is the most appropriate response I could give to my child and the situation at this moment?"

For example, a child might be fearful of going to a party because they are not so sure about what they are going to experience, who they are going to meet, or where it is taking place. This is a completely natural human response for some children, and indeed adults. Telling them not to worry undermines their thoughts and feelings. Asking them, "What do you need right now to help?" may be a more gentle and conscious approach to a situation, which is anxiety-provoking for them.

When our children are frightened, frustrated and finding it hard to make sense of a situation it is important to acknowledge their thoughts and feelings. Asking ourselves, "What is the most conscious way that I can respond to how they are feeling?" helps us relate to them in such a way that our children feel listened to, valued and understood.

Greater understanding

The calm, connected and conscious "Why Parent" process has helped bring me to a greater understanding of my instinct, heart and brain. It has ultimately helped me have a better relationship with my children.

Reflecting on why we do what we do through being calm, connected and conscious helps us as parents in all situations, whether we are feeling overwhelmed or happy.

We need to connect in a way that suits our child in that moment

Just as there are many different ways of learning there are many different ways of developing our relationships with our children. Many of us have lost confidence as parents because we feel we need to look for answers from experts such as Super Nanny, Dr Spock, Dr Sears and Gina Ford.

Parents' confidence and self-esteem seem to be inversely proportional to the amount written about parenting. There is so much conflicting information and advice, so many techniques, such as putting children on a "naughty step" or giving rewards and stickers to our children. These are a behaviourist tick-box approach to parenting; a nurturing approach is to trust our emotions and ask our children what they need.

Many children feel very threatened with fear-based behaviourist approaches such as "time out"; it is counterintuitive and counterproductive to threaten a child who is trying to make sense of their emotions and feelings.

What children really crave is to be valued, understood and listened to; what is the long-term value in punishment and love-withdrawal? I am sure as adults we might react in a defensive way to a boss suddenly putting "reward charts" on the staffroom fridge door and having a "time out" chair in the office.

Consider the perspective of the child

The bottom line is to consider the perspective of the child. Ask yourself, "How would I feel if I was on the receiving end of what I just said or did? What would I believe about myself if that were said or done to me? What would my response be?"

As parents, our focus is to develop our relationships with our children and connect with them rather than micro-manage their behaviour.

For many parents there is a lack of confidence and disconnection with ourselves, which our children are picking up. Our job is to repair that disconnection somehow, learn to trust our instincts. Parenting materials become our security blanket when we feel we are not good enough, or when we try to be perfect parents.

The best way we can help our children is to model our connection with ourselves, and then to step up, be authentic and allow them to be who they need to be.

Letting go of our own parents' parenting style

Sometimes it is tempting to blame the way we were parented for the way we are parenting our own children. This can be quite disabling and can be a block in our relationship with our children.

Blaming our past experiences, thinking, "I am not good enough as a parent because of what my father did or what my mum said" prevents us from being the best parents we can be. Instead, we need to choose more empowering thoughts and beliefs about our parenting.

We can choose to liberate ourselves from our past and think about who we need to be now. We can choose what we say and do with our children right now. It doesn't have to be a psychoanalytical approach; it is a simple choice. We can be dragged down by our past or become hijacked into worrying about what is going to happen in the future, or we can choose something new, now.

It is possible to change the way we think and act

Expert thinking about our ability to impact on our thoughts and beliefs has radically changed in the last few years. Neuro-scientific research has shown that the brain's neuroplasticity and ability to form new connections means that we can instantaneously change our thoughts and belief systems if we allow ourselves to do so.

Feelings of guilt, shame and confusion can stop us from being the parents we want to be. In my role as a teacher and psychologist I have had the privilege of meeting hundreds of parents, and I have met many parents who blame themselves for the way their children are and want to "fix" the child or the situation.

What I do in my role is help acknowledge the experiences from the past that make us who we are.

Creating positive parenting stories gives us the strength and inner resources to face challenging situations in the now and in the future.

Past experiences – whether they are perceived as good or bad – can help us as parents and can be gifts to our children.

If as parents we are experiencing feelings of guilt, shame and confusion, these are action points to do something about. We need to allow ourselves to feel them and then move past them in order to be who we need to be for our children.

Letting go of anxiety about the future

I also meet parents (and have been one myself) whose thoughts are paralysed by focusing on the future. They are anxious about the future and much of what they do is based on what they think will help their children get on in life. This seems to dominate modern parenting.

Parents might think they need to take their child to music lessons when actually the child has shown no interest in music, because parents feel it is a good thing for kids to learn.

It is much healthier to just enjoy what they show us they love doing right now. Our children's strengths and interests evolve much more authentically if they are given a chance to grow organically rather than being "genetically modified" by artificially accelerating them.

As parents we sometimes get anxious about what we "should" be doing for our children and put them into swimming lessons just because we think it is a good thing to do. Of course, being safe in the water is a useful life skill to have! Our children need to learn how to be safe in water but there are other ways of helping them learn how to swim rather than formal lessons.

Ultimately our children are not checklists to be ticked off. When they show us that they are ready for certain experiences, that is the moment to enjoy learning-milestone experiences together. We can get so entrenched in the past and in thinking about the future that we lose the best part of parenting, which is our children right here, right now, in front of us.

The school system

The same could be said of the school system, which is obsessed with preparing our children for the "next stage" of education, whatever that may be. I like the definition of education as being "drawing out what is from within."

My feeling is that education is being perceived by our children as "filling them with skills to get to the next level."

When I asked Fred what he thought the purpose of school was, he said, "Getting you ready for secondary school." I was saddened to think that our children are picking up belief systems that school is about getting ready for the next stage of schooling rather than enjoying a lifelong-learning journey in the moment.

As parents, we, too, may be falling into the trap of preparing children for the next stage instead of seeing them for who they are now.

To be fair, later on in the conversation Fred also said school was about, "Making me a better person." I would like to think that schools are mirroring this desire of children and parents to be well-rounded, balanced people rather than national-curriculum-level junkies.

When we get lost in the past or the future, we miss the greatest moments, those that are happening now.

The most important message I have for parents is: enjoy the moment.

Why The Why Parent?

The Why Parent, my parenting journey, and my desire to help other parents, evolved from three major turning points in my life.

The first trigger was my father leaving the family home when I was seven. There was not a lot of discussion within the family about why that happened. Indeed, there was not a lot of discussion about how that made everybody in the family feel.

Being the youngest of three girls, I saw my eldest sister cope with the situation by going out, partying and being with her friends. My middle sister would stay in her room, immersing herself in schoolwork and playing the piano.

I tended to take a back seat and observe rather than participate and felt detached from family life. I do not ever remember being asked how I felt about the situation. Maybe that is just a sign of the times, growing up in the 1970s with adults not knowing how to ask such questions of children, or possibly not wanting to hear the answers.

In the work I do as a psychologist I am very conscious that if you do not explore feelings at the time it can lead to emotions being raised later that are difficult to process. Being able to explain what you are thinking and how you feel helps you understand and make sense of any situation.

Regardless of whether it is a traumatic, anxious, or indeed a happy time, expressing emotions supports developing a deeper understanding of your life story. Having opportunities to discuss how you feel helps you make sense of yourself and your place in the world.

The motivator for me to create The Why Parent was to help children and parents make sense of their emotions and their relationship in any situation.

The second trigger for The Why Parent was my experience as a teacher. I found teaching both demanding and stimulating. Sometimes we have life experiences that provide an overwhelmingly accelerated learning curve. Teaching was a privilege and also one of those experiences.

I was given the opportunity to teach in a village school as well as an inner-London urban environment. I ultimately felt I wanted to understand the learning process at a deeper level. As a teacher in a class of thirty children, I felt I was policing, managing behaviour and organizing rather than being able to connect with and teach the children on an individual basis.

That feeling of frustration as a teacher led me to train as an educational psychologist, to see what difference I could make with a deeper understanding of how children learn.

Honouring feelings over parental expectations

At the same time as I was training to be a teacher I met my now husband, Av. He is from a Sikh background and there was an expectation from his family that Av would have an arranged marriage to a Sikh girl.

As a white Christian from Yorkshire I did not exactly fit the bill, and this raised questions for me: "What is marriage all about? Why would a parent choose their child's partner? What is being a parent all about if you do not want your child to be happy?" It seemed to me that this was about parental expectation rather than love.

I have the greatest admiration for Av, being authentic and honouring his feelings over parental expectations. He is the strongest person I know.

After years of trying to have our own family we had our first child, Fred, through IVF. I then discovered I was pregnant with Tom who was conceived naturally when Fred was six months old. In fifteen months I had two children. This was an amazing gift but also incredibly overwhelming and the third trigger in my journey as a parent and creating The Why Parent.

I was not prepared for my emotions

Even with my experience as a teacher and psychologist, I was not prepared for the immense feelings of being a new parent: out of control, frustrated and confused. Different midwives, health visitors, doctors, family and friends bombarded me with both goodwill and advice.

I remember one day hiding behind the sofa as the doorbell rang, knowing the health visitor was due to arrive. I was hiding because I felt a failure as a parent. I was asking very disempowering questions such as, "What am I doing wrong?" "Am I doing enough for my child?"

Several years later the feeling of disempowerment and depression still continued and I knew I needed to do something about it.

Fred's question

A defining moment for me came at the time when Fred was starting school. One sunny September morning he asked me, "Why do I have to go to school?"

Our children ask us "why" all the time and although adults find it tiring to always answer the "why", I welcomed the question. **I wanted to take the "why" seriously.** Why do you have to go to school? Why do I have to go to work? Why do parents feel guilty, shame and confused? Why do our children begin to mirror our guilt, shame and confusion?

I welcomed the "why" because it helped me go back to first principles.

We naturally focus on the "what" we do and "how" we do it as parents, but I wanted to know my "why." I founded The Why Parent to help other parents find their why.

Fred's question helped me reflect on the basic fundamental assumptions that we make and collude with as adults without question. I handed over my child to the education system and I did not really know what he was experiencing. It was uncomfortable for me to rethink the fundamental concept of education – I had a degree in teaching, and still I was struggling.

At the same time as Fred was starting school I was working in my role as an educational psychologist on a traumatic case. I was working with guardians of a child who had witnessed a horrific incident as a baby. He was now twelve years old and had been under the care of various professionals and agencies. Communication between the different agencies was limited and the child and the guardians were desperate for support.

The child was displaying extremely risky, challenging behaviour and I felt the other professionals were observing what was happening and not intervening because they were unsettled by his behaviour. The guardians were left to deal with the fallout and were feeling very isolated.

I asked myself, "What is my role and how can I support this child when all the other professionals are backing off?" At the same time I was asking myself, "What is my role as a parent?"

The over-riding question was, "What am I here for?" Not only as a professional working with the child and guardians, attempting to help them through a very challenging time, but also as a parent of a child starting school.

I had an overwhelming sense of not knowing what to expect as a parent of my child in school and I was questioning what my role was. The irony was that I had visited hundreds of schools in my role as a teacher and psychologist. The new relationship with my son's school was confusing, as I felt I "should" know what my role would be.

I came up with the concept of The Why Parent to help me through a process of understanding my own situation, and also to help other parents who were going through the same thing, and who were feeling isolated or overwhelmed, who felt they didn't have the information they needed to make choices and decisions on behalf of their children.

What do you want for your children?

When I ask parents what they want children to be they come up with words such as "happy," "healthy," "caring," "sociable," "creative," "independent," "resilient." I have not had a parent say they want their child to be a number in the National Curriculum.

For the majority of parents I meet, the focus is on having happy and healthy children. Having healthy and happy children comes from having healthy and happy parents in healthy and happy communities. We need people and communities that are working, consciously and actively, towards health and happiness at an individual, family, school and community level.

This is how we can help society become calm, connected and conscious. We can start, as Gandhi says, to "be the change" we want to see.

Being a "Why Parent" is about understanding ourselves, our past experiences and how we have been parented. This helps us gain a deeper understanding of our beliefs, feelings and thoughts, so we can choose to be who we want to be as a parent.

When we are authentic and know who we are, we can have a greater connection with our children.

Parents are the first teachers

Parents are the first teachers of their children and I would like parents to feel empowered to work in parallel with schools to help their children be the best that they can be; and to acknowledge that they have that role.

I support parents by coaching them individually and in groups, in the community and in schools.

Working with parents in groups within a school setting is a powerful way of working so that schools and parents are talking the same language for the same ends: healthy and happy children.

The process of having a calm, connected and conscious approach to our parenting in order to have an amazing relationship with our children is a focus of The Why Parent.

The rest of this book delves into The Why Parent approach, exploring nine essential elements to having a healthy and happy relationship with our children:

W - wellbeing

H - happiness

Y- you

P - positivity

A - attachment

R - resilience

E - enjoyment

N - now

T – thanks

Activity – exploring you as a parent

Take a few minutes to consider the following question. If you like, you can jot down your thoughts.

What were the triggers in your life that make you the amazing parent you are today? (these events or situations when you reflect on them create your parenting story, your gift to your children)

This is '**Parentuality**,' the way we connect with our parenting story, ourselves, our children, and life.

Parentuality		
Wellbeing **H**appiness **Y**ou	**P**ositivity **A**ttachment **R**esilience	**E**njoyment **N**ow **T**hanks
Connecting with Self	*Connecting with Child*	*Connecting with Life*

CHAPTER TWO
WELLBEING

> *"The attitude that you have as a parent is what your kids will learn from, more than what you tell them. They don't remember what you try to teach them. They remember what you are."*
>
> Jim Henson

Wellbeing is a fundamental key to our parenting. I have been guilty as anybody else of feeling the "need" to just keep going with the business of work and the demands of being a parent without paying attention to what I needed myself.

At an energetic, emotional and physical level, parenting really takes it out of us. We are doing our children a disservice if we do not look after ourselves and take care of our physical and emotional wellbeing. As parents we also need to take care of our minds. It is a fundamental truth that mind and body and spirit closely interact.

Being a role model for our children is vital. Children do what we do rather than what we say. If they see that we are not eating in a way that is conducive to wellbeing then they are going to pick up those habits. Taking care of our bodies at a cellular level is important.

I used to be addicted to fizzy drinks and did not realise it (or maybe did not want to acknowledge it!) until I met a wellness coach who analysed what I ate and drank. It was a shock for me that even being over forty years of age I had not made the link between my mood and the food I was eating.

Those sneaky petrol station pasties and fizzy drinks filled with sweeteners while I was driving around between school visits as an educational psychologist were contributing to my downward mood.

It hit home recently how far I had shifted my habits when Fred noticed a rare can of Diet Coke in the car cup holder. "I thought you had given up fizzy drinks," he observed.

"I thought I had too," I confessed. *A temporary relapse!*

Our children are more likely to do what we do rather than what we say we do or tell them to do.

Taking care of ourselves at a cellular level

There is a body of research from Bruce Lipton and Daniel Amen that looks at why we need to really take care of ourselves at a cellular level. Our cells, and therefore our whole bodies, are made of water, protein and fatty acids. It makes sense that eating protein and drinking water are really important to sustain our cells.

Children need to be given information about nutrition from an early age in order to make informed choices. I remember in biology at school being given information about digestion and a balanced diet, but not really the facts about the science of nutrition at a chemical and cellular level.

The public outlook has changed. There is the message of "Five fruit and vegetables a day," "Healthy Schools" initiatives and Jamie Oliver's school dinner campaigns. It is fundamental: at a chemical level what we eat and drink affects our energy levels, health, moods and therefore how we show up as parents.

Sleep

It feels great when we have at least eight hours of sleep. Parenting becomes challenging when we are sleep-deprived. It is hard to give a calm, connected and conscious response to our children when our sleep needs have not been met.

Sleep is so important because when we are in sleep-deprivation mode the "fight or flight" feeling in the brain stem trigger kicks in a lot quicker; the fear response triggers more readily and we are less likely to produce that conscious question or response.

Exercise

Exercise releases endorphins and oxytocin, which help us feel good. We are in a better place to respond positively to our children when our energy levels are high, so that when they ask us to go out and play a game of football with them we can say "Yes" because we want to play, be physical and present with our children.

What does the child need?

It is much easier to problem solve a situation when my children tell me what it is that they need. It is amazing that as children they are able to state what they need – it is such an important life skill.

I think sometimes as adults we just carry on without asking, "What do I need now?" Parents might say that it is self-indulgent to say what we need.

There is a distinction to be made between what a child needs versus what they want. A child may say, "I want the latest Lego model" and this is different from what they need, which might be a connection, a smile, or a hug, to feel valued and needed. If children get their basic emotional needs met they are less likely to want a continuous stream of toys.

Meeting our own needs first

Sometimes we are intolerant of what our children need because we feel frustrated that our needs are not being met. **If our needs are met we are more likely to meet the needs of our children.**

Fostering our own wellbeing is such an important value and gift to give our children. We sometimes feel guilty planning time for us. It is not selfish to say, "I need to go for a swim, a run, or meet a friend for coffee". In fact, if we state what it is that we need, that helps our children understand that it is okay to articulate needs and wants and they learn to do so, too. That is part of being human.

If we ask the question as a parent, "What do I need?" the answer might be, a ten minute power nap, a walk, meditation, or to read a book. This is not a bad question to ask if it results in us being in a better place to look after our children emotionally, physically and mentally. We can lose sight of our own needs as parents and asking the question, "What do I need?" really helps.

We are more able to appreciate our family when we have had some time to recuperate and rejuvenate. If we ignore what our body and mind need, it can build to feelings of resentment and frustration, which ultimately our children begin to pick up on and model.

Our needs evolve

If I asked myself at twenty, "What do I need and what makes me happy?" it would be a very different answer to what the answer is now. What we need and what makes us happy evolves.

Sometimes we expect our partners and children to know by osmosis what we are thinking or feeling, but they may have no idea unless we state what it is that we need.

Having our own friends

Being sociable and connecting with our own friends is really important for ourselves and so that children see us as role models, having friendships - they see us playing at our level. Play is important for parents well as for our children. Einstein wisely stated, "Play is the highest form of research."

Simply enjoying the moment

It is fabulous watching a child playing with a balloon and this is something we can learn from as adults. It is the most pleasurable experience in that moment! The delight of exploring something, catching bubbles, digging mud with a stick or playing with an empty cardboard box.

Whatever it might be, just knowing what we need is really important and sometimes we do not take time to stand back and reflect on that.

Self-awareness tool - journaling

Journaling helps me to think about what I am feeling and thinking. It focuses my understanding of what I have enjoyed, what has made me happy, as well as what I have been frustrated by and what I have learned.

The process of writing helps me reflect on what I need. I know if I do not have some quiet time to reflect during the day I get frustrated and begin to feel overwhelmed.

It may be that journaling would be a useful tool for you to connect more with yourself.

Activity

Try spending some time each day writing in a journal. What you write is not important – just getting your thoughts out of your head and down on paper can make all the difference.

Everybody is different

Listen to your body and mind and ask, "What do I need emotionally, physically and spiritually?" This is an individual thing. Only you know what you need to make you happy.

It is not for me to say what you need or what your child needs. These are not going to be the same things I need or my children need.

In my work I ask questions to help parents reflect on what they and their children need to be joyful, happy, content and have a deeper understanding of each other.

Activity

Get into the habit of regularly asking yourself, "What do I need now?" – and also asking your children, "What do you need?" This helps enormously to develop self-awareness. Start with once a day until it becomes second-nature.

Personal styles

Some people are very kinesthetic or physical and enjoy being outside gardening, walking or going for a run. Physicality is very important to make them happy and to raise endorphins and energy levels.

Other people are very logical and like problem-solving as a way of relaxing and being in the moment.

Some people like visual stimulation: computers, films and television, to relax.

Others are auditory and love to listen to information or music.

As parents we need to be authentic and connect with ourselves in order to have better connections with our children. It is important that we know our children's learning style and what they need in that moment.

Sitting back and observing

Sometimes we find it difficult to sit back and observe our children. We interject and jump in. We want to fix and solve their problems for them instead of allowing them to explore and just be happy in the moment.

If you're not practiced at this, try just watching and observing your children in free play, in that creative moment – whether their style is auditory, physical, or visual – as they just explore an object. Watch without judging what they are doing. Let their actions wash over you and watch for the emotions and feelings they are creating.

I remember a situation recently when I was guilty of being the parent "fun police" in the park. The boys were playing table tennis on an outdoor table and they had invented their own game.

I asked a question about what the score went up to and what the rules were. They had come up with their own game and I had instantaneously burst their metaphorical bubble by mentioning "scores and rules". They decided they didn't want to play that game anymore and went off to play something else.

That is what we sometimes do as adults. We interject too much and micromanage instead of letting children just be themselves.

As adults, we can connect with simple mundane pleasures, from making the tea, ironing, dusting and – my personal favourite – cleaning the inside of the car! Those jobs that we sometimes think are tedious can be wonderful moments if we allow them to be. How we approach and choose to think of those moments is the key. They can be just empty moments with not much happening, or we can fill them with meaning.

A comedy about nothing

The creators of *Seinfeld* – one of the greatest television situation comedies of all time – took great pleasure in creating "a comedy about nothing". The programme might have appeared to have no real storyline as it portrayed the lives of four characters hanging out together in New York. What was interesting was that the "nothing" was always "something" and the simplicity of focusing on the relationships between the characters was comedy genius.

Empty down-time can be the most memorable in terms of developing our relationships with our children.

Process over achievement

Sometimes as a society we give more status to keeping busy and to achievements than to enjoying the process; we do not celebrate the process as much as we could. We put pressure on ourselves to deliver outcomes on which we feel we will ultimately be judged.

My view is that life is a journey. Cleaning out the car can be the most monotonous task in the world but it can also be an opportunity to have some reflection time, during which light bulb moments can occur. Then it actually can be a moment of joy. We choose whether to think of it as a chore or as an opportunity.

Reflection:

"*Communal wellbeing is central to human life.*"

Cat Stevens

Activity: Your wellbeing

Give yourself a "wellbeing" rating from 1 to 10 (with 10 being the best it could be)

My wellbeing rating _____

What would raising the rating by just one look like? What would your partner, children, friend notice if you were one higher?

CHAPTER THREE
HAPPINESS

===

"Happiness is when what you think, what you say, and what you do are in harmony."

Mahatma Gandhi

How can we really connect with our children and help them to be happy and healthy?

Were you ever taught how to be happy? I am guessing the answer is "no" – you have never been consciously taught how to be happy.

If we want happy and healthy children we need to be happy and healthy adults. Increasing numbers of children have mental health difficulties; we need to look at ourselves as parents and how we are showing up, in terms of our happiness levels. Demonstrating good models of happiness to our children is the ideal.

I knew that in order to be a better parent I needed to work on my own mental health. I needed to begin by understanding why I said and did things to my children that I really did not want to say or do.

Judgement in society

The Why Parent approach is a positive process, which focuses on the values of wellbeing and happiness rather than on judgement. Our society has a lot of negativity and judgement through newspapers, television, magazines and the general media. Our children have only really experienced what I call the "X-Factor generation", where people are judged and voted in or out.

"Big Brother", "Britain's Got Talent", "I'm a Celebrity get me out of here", "Strictly Come Dancing": there is a generation in our society that has grown up with the idea that it is okay to judge people by text or phone. In the process they are also judging themselves.

There is also a generation of children that has gone through the education system of the National Curriculum from 1989; they are now in their thirties and have grown up with having to make the expected level, being judged and in many cases not feeling "good enough".

On another level, while social media undoubtedly brings people together, it can also be a vehicle for parents and children to feel judged. It is worrying that many children are growing up without developing an understanding of who they are as individuals because the social norm is to compare and judge ourselves alongside other people.

When we compare and judge ourselves against other people it distances us from what we are truly feeling and thinking. Are we feeling joy, sadness, fear or anger or are we just pretending to fit into a group?

A range of emotions is really important to not only be aware of and articulate, but also to truly feel. If children feel they have to conform to what everyone else is thinking and feeling that does not help them understand who they are; they are then more vulnerable to peer pressure and are more likely to experiment with risky behaviour in order to conform to the group.

Developing empathy

Children are more likely to have a strong sense of empathy and take someone else's perspective when their own emotional needs are being met – and that is more likely when their parent's needs are also being met. If we understand ourselves better we have more empathy for our friends and family and a greater understanding of what we can contribute to society.

Many parents I meet know that they want to go from a feeling of frustration to happiness and calm. They are not quite sure what the process is to take the first step of the journey, but they know they want to start.

For me, parenting is about giving ourselves permission to understand who we are and step into our joy, which ultimately is an endless gift we can give to our children.

Activity

Check in with your emotions right now, and write down what you are feeling here. Doing this on a regular basis is another way to connect with the deeper part of you.

Ask your child, "How are you feeling right now?" Write their response here. Some children find it hard to articulate their feelings but might find it easier to articulate "what are you thinking?"

Were your parents comfortable talking about emotions?

How we were parented ourselves impacts on what we say and do to our children. I come from a generation where often our parents felt uncomfortable talking about how they felt. I don't remember ever being asked by my parents to talk about how I felt. Maybe it is selective memory but I do not remember my parents really talking about how *they* felt about a situation they were experiencing. They may have talked about the practicalities of "what" or "how" but not how they really felt.

Being parented in that way as a child I might have concluded that "feelings are taboo and I am not allowed to feel certain emotions because that's too scary," or "I am not allowed to be angry, sad or frustrated" because that would make my parents feel uncomfortable. I felt I needed to conform so that I did not rock the proverbial boat.

I remember seeing in the park a parent shouting, "Stop crying" to a two-year-old child. They carried on with, "Stop crying and I'll give you a biscuit."

Crying is what children need to do in order to learn how to regulate their feelings. Children have big emotions and sometimes those emotions are expressed as crying. Crying is a basic human response and if we give our children the message they have to stop, they may conclude that "I am not allowed to cry – crying is bad."

Giving food or drink to help calm a situation usually only helps to reduce the adult's fear response. It doesn't meet the immediate need of the child: to feel understood, valued and validated, and ultimately to know that it is ok to have big emotions.

As adults we are there to help them understand what they are feeling and why they might be feeling that emotion. Children are not always able to articulate how they are thinking and feeling. Crying is a very human way of expressing that.

If we haven't learned to be okay with our own emotions, we won't be able to help our children deal with theirs; or we may dismiss the crying because it does not fit in to our time schedule. In either case, children conclude that it is not acceptable to have a big emotion and to cry. They therefore learn strategies to not truly feel and express emotions and begin to mistrust their feelings.

Handling our own emotions

As parents we need to be able to regulate our own emotional response. If we are not sure how to handle our emotions then this is being modelled to our toddlers through to teenagers. It is okay to have these very strong emotions, but at times we are not able to articulate them. We might be verbally or physically aggressive, sarcastic or take it out on a cold caller!

We need to teach ourselves how to experience our own emotions in a safe, appropriate way; then we can demonstrate this to our children. How we demonstrate our emotions is the key. If we show there is a way to have strong emotions safely, we can talk about how it feels and model this approach. It helps our children believe it is safe to have big emotions.

It is useful to take on board the idea of stepping into and feeling emotions. Think about the last time you cried. What would you have wanted someone to have said or done to help you when you were crying?

Ask your child what he or she needs

Everybody is different in how we respond to a big emotion. If we ask our children what they need to help them, rather than judging and imposing our way of trying to solve the problem, then our children will know their feelings are being understood and validated rather than being undermined.

When our children are given a message "don't be scared/frightened/sad", their feelings then become moments of threat and fear rather than a useful release.

If we rush children through their big feelings it may send out implicit messages that they have to hide their emotions; they may become scared about the adult's response to an expression of feelings.

Excitement and joy

I wonder how often we also let our children feel complete excitement and joy before we hurry them on to the next activity.

I remember when Fred won a high kick championship in Taekwondo. The look of pure elation on his face was a joy. He jumped up and down and punched the air; but instead of me sharing in that moment, I was embarrassed, thinking, "He looks like he's showing off."

I was thinking how other parents and children would perceive this moment of victory instead of being with Fred in that moment. I did not know how to handle my child's celebration. I realised that this reflected part of my belief system about achievement. As I child, I was told to be quiet and not boast or brag about my achievements.

As John Wayne said, "It ain't bragging if you can do it." Once I knew where the judgemental thought was coming from, I had the sense to "park" it somewhere in order to help Fred celebrate his moment and feel his sense of pride.

What were things like for you as a child?

On reflection, the language I remember as a child was very practical and functional in order to get through the day; there was little or no talking about thoughts and feelings.

When I talk to parents, the general picture I get is that awareness about emotional literacy was not great for our parents' generation.

So how can we move through that from the collective consciousness of a past generation of parents, who either Were not aware of or found it hard to be able to explore emotions, to a new generation of children who have far more opportunities to talk about their emotions and feelings? It's up to us to make that change.

Reflection:

"*Happiness is not ready made. It comes from your own actions.*"

Dalai Lama

Activity: your happiness

Give yourself a "happiness" rating from 1 to 10 (with 10 being the best it could be)

My happiness rating _____

What would raising the rating by just one look like? What would your partner, children, friend notice if you were one more?

CHAPTER FOUR

YOU

_____

"When someone shows you who they are,
believe them the first time."

Maya Angelou

The most important aspect of being a parent is being
true to yourself and true to your children – bringing
you to your role as parent. What is important to you?
What do you value? What sort of a home, and what
sort of world do you want your children to grow up
in? This chapter is about reflecting your values and
beliefs in your parenting.

Values as a key to relationships
_____

Understanding our values is the key to relationships
and connection with our children. I do not mean
values in terms of a political or religious connotation
of values. I am talking about values from a sense of
focusing on what is most important to you in your
life with your family.

At a Labour Party conference, Ed Milliband talked about his values of "One Nation" by retelling the story of how his family were immigrants and were welcomed into a tolerant Britain working to rebuild the country following the Second World War. That value of working together as a team for one vision is not necessarily a political message but an ideal that I am sure we would all like our children and communities to have.

If as a family one of our values is, "We work collaboratively as a team", it is much easier to be consistent about what we say and do with our children by focusing on being a team.

In working to understand myself I found I needed to be honest about exploring my personal parenting story, asking myself, "What are my values?" "Where does that behaviour come from?" "Why do I say and do those things to my children?"

Destruction can fulfil a need

Sometimes we can impose our values on our children, rather than allowing them to make their own choices. For example, if a child chooses to screw up a drawing we need to find out what they are thinking in order to understand that destroying their work fulfils a need. We might be tempted instead to tell them off, in effect telling them it is not okay to do this – but that doesn't help what is going on inside.

Feeling so frustrated that they need to throw it in the bin – that thinking comes from their emotions. Their emotions come from their beliefs about themselves. It could be their belief system is "I am not good enough", "I am rubbish at drawing", "everything I do is wrong." Their value about themselves impacts on beliefs, which directly affect emotions and feelings, leading to the observable behaviour of throwing their work in the bin.

It may be that children are concluding that they are "not good enough", in an education system where there is a predicted "norm" that a child has to meet.

If this norm is not met then the child by implication is not "good enough" and may feel that they are not valued.

What are your values?

If we can really understand where our values come from, whether they were given to us, or acquired along the way, then we are more able to support our children in developing their own values and beliefs.

Activity

What values were you given as a child?

What values would you like to give to your child?

A positive value that I was given as a child was that working hard and doing well at school were important. For me, education was a means to being able to make choices about what I wanted to do with my life.

Our school's motto was: "Whatever I do, I do to the best of my ability." This has stood me in good stead to do my best with the skills and inner resources that I have.

I do not feel the need to compare myself to others because I grew up with a belief system that working hard, education and health were important in order to do what you want to do in life. I never felt the need to compete with anyone else.

Understanding what our values are and where they are coming from is fundamental to being conscious about what we say and what we do with our children.

If we were brought up in a situation where we were controlled or neglected or not really understood, that may have led to a negative set of values and beliefs being learned. Being brought up in an environment where we were valued and acknowledged may have established a more positive set of values and beliefs, which would result in different behaviours. Whatever the case, it is always possible to choose our own values for the future.

Parenting is not a test

Some parents have a notion that parenting is about "being right." I remember a particular parent, Jo, who felt frustrated because she thought she was "getting it wrong." Jo's metaphor for her parenting – the way she understood it – was that parenting is a test. As a lawyer, Jo saw life in terms of right or wrong. It is a natural instinct to take these skills into parenting. The work we did together was to challenge the notion that parenting is about getting it "right or wrong."

What do you think? Is that the truth? Do we want to pass on to our children the idea that "life is a test"? Can we reframe parenting by thinking life is more than being "right or wrong"?

If we ask ourselves questions such as, "What should I say in this situation?" or, "What should I do?" these are quite disempowering questions as they imply there is a right or wrong answer. A more empowering question might be: "How can I support my child in this situation?" or, "What do they need right now?"

What is your parenting metaphor?

If you ask yourself about your own parenting metaphor, and get to understand it, you can see whether or not it is empowering you – and change it, if you would like to.

Working with Jo was really interesting; she decided that instead of seeing parenting as a "test" it could be a "game" to be enjoyed and learned from. It helped all the parents in the parenting group she was part of to realise there are no right answers in parenting: there are great lessons to be learned.

We are all learning from each other and one of the joys of being a parent is discovering something new about ourselves and our children every day.

This is a powerful process for parents, asking ourselves: What have I learned about myself and my child today? How am I a better parent than I was yesterday? These are much more empowering questions than, "Why am I getting it wrong?"

We can choose to feel guilty and beat ourselves up about what we are not doing, or we can ask, "What helped, what did I learn, what could I do next time?

Understanding and choosing our metaphor of parenting

Having a parenting metaphor will provide a lifelong tool to understand our children at a deeper level and ultimately have an amazing relationship with them.

At another level, our values tend to transfer to our children – it is important that we work to understand our children's values and beliefs, as well as our own.

Our children absorb the values, beliefs, thoughts and feelings that we co-create with them. If we model to our children that we value life-long learning, being authentic and that we learn from mistakes, then their beliefs, emotions and behaviour will also reflect this value system.

If we believe it is okay to have emotions, they are likely also to have this belief.

Understanding where our values come from and acknowledging, appreciating and nurturing them helps us know what our end goal is as a family and can make a big difference to our parenting. Discovering this is an important piece of work as a parent: finding out what our values are at a subconscious level. That subconscious mindset controls our behaviour.

Scientists argue over the figures about just how much of our behaviour is conscious versus subconscious; the growing consensus seems to be that around 95% of what we do is controlled by our subconscious and 5% by our conscious self.

We can either reject the values that we were given when we were parented or we can embrace them. There is a synergy combining those early "blueprint" values and what we have learned through our own experiences. We can either resist those early values or see them as a gift. If we really understand where our values are coming from it helps us connect at a subconscious level with our children. If we identify and then actively choose our values, we can make sure that what we are saying and what we are doing as parents is congruent with what is important to us. Our values and beliefs are the "why" of our parenting.

A good place to start in moving towards more calm, conscious and connected parenting is to work through your values and beliefs, and to think about what your metaphor for parenting is. Parenting may be seen as a "gift" or a "joy" or it can be a "challenge" a "game" or a "struggle". Articulating what parenting is for you is important because it is the starting point from which to explore your values.

Once we are aware of what our metaphor of parenting is, it gives us clarity and focus on what we do and say to our children. Everybody's metaphor is different; we all have a unique way of looking at parenting, which begins with our individual life experiences.

Begin to think about what your metaphor for parenting is. When you think about the phrase, "Parenting is …," what immediately comes to mind? We'll do a full activity about this later. For the moment, just begin to revolve the idea of your parenting metaphor in your mind.

The first time I did this exercise I came up with the parenting metaphor of "resistance like a block in an electrical circuit" – that I would meet resistance as a parent. This explained my moments of frustration when I was greeted with a "no," or when I felt I was not being listened to. I realised this wasn't how I wanted it to be.

What do you want?

Once you see what your current metaphor for parenting is, think about whether this is how you want it to be. Is there something you would prefer to have as a metaphor instead?

I realised that what I wanted was a calm family home where everyone listened and valued each other.

It wasn't surprising that I was getting frustrated. Focusing on what I wanted family life to be like helped me create a more positive perspective.

Part of my anger was coming from not feeling listened to or valued myself, and understanding this helped me empathise with my children when I could see that they also might be feeling this way. Meeting what I saw as "resistance" with love and acceptance and not frustration was the key for me to change. When I stared to accept and love myself the resistance stopped.

How understanding our parenting metaphor helps

Articulating our parenting metaphors provides clarity to why we might raise our voice, or get annoyed about a toy on the floor. Our automatic responses often come from our childhood. It is in those moments of responding automatically that it is useful to ask, "Where did that come from?"

There are lots of examples I can think of when I have had a moment of complete terror after saying something that had been stored from the way I was parented myself.

I remember asking myself, "Why did I get so upset when the Lego was all over the floor?" I realised I was thinking, "That is an expensive piece of Lego kit and it is all over the floor." Growing up with one Lego set and a family of five Lego figures, I always made sure that all the precious pieces were accounted for. That spilled over, and it worried me that my children were not grateful for their toys, or careful of them – my issue, not theirs.

In reality, Lego is there to be enjoyed and to be mixed up. Lego sets are not created to get parents upset over the fact that it might get all mixed up together. The irony is that Lego means "play well" in Danish and I was getting anxious about where the pieces were escaping to!

We sometimes retreat to an adult agenda in our heads, and it is useful to ask ourselves, "Where is that value and belief coming from?" and "Is this how I want to be?"

The metaphor is a helpful way of thinking. We can choose whatever metaphor we like. If we have a metaphor that parenting is a gift, then it is something to be opened, cherished and unwrapped. There are layers that can be discovered. Changing our metaphor changes our actions and words.

Where do your values and beliefs come from?

It is thought-provoking work to acknowledge where values and beliefs originate. To be authentic as a parent and totally connected with our children we need to do that work to connect with ourselves. Understanding where our parenting metaphor comes from allows us to move forward and make active choices about how we want to be. It can transform our relationship with ourselves and our children.

Whatever the metaphor, whether it's, "Parenting is a gift to be unwrapped and discovered" or,

"Parenting is an adventure to be explored", or "parenting is a game," our metaphor is unique to each one of us.

I have worked with parents who have said that parenting for them is "noise" or "chaos". If we walk through life thinking and believing that "parenting is chaos" then what we say and do with our children will be chaotic. Our children feel our energy and they pick up on the chaotic thinking. Taking time and space to reflect on that can help us change not only the way we see our parenting but also how we see ourselves.

We can use it as an excuse that "parenting is chaotic," or we can say as one parent did, "I want to get rid of chaos and replace it with "parenting is calm. I want my family life to be calm. I want my home to have an atmosphere that my children can feel safe and secure and can grow up being the best they can be."

Activity: my parenting metaphor

What is your current parenting metaphor? Spend some time thinking about this, or go with the first impression that comes to mind.

My current parenting metaphor:

parenting is _____

(e.g. an adventure, a challenge, a joy, a ...)

Think back through your life, particularly the way you were parented, and see if you can identify where this metaphor came from. Write your insights here:

Is this metaphor working well for you? Does it help you create the life and relationship you want for you and your children?

What is your ideal vision of family life? What does it look and feel like? Take some time for this and think about how you would really like it to be ...

What would a more powerful parenting metaphor be for you? How would you ideally like to see parenting:

My new parenting metaphor:

parenting is _____

What would be your family motto or mantra be?

Having a family motto or mantra is a way of values being articulated collectively and openly. It can be a very positive thing to work with your partner and children to come up with a family motto.

Activity

Set aside some time to work out your family motto.

Our vision for our lives

Once we as parents, and also as a family, articulate a phrase for our vision for our lives it really helps us step up to be better parents. It helps us to improve our relationships with our children. Even just doing this exercise can help transform family lives.

As parents we do not tend to protect that reflection time to ask what do we want from our parenting and families? What would it be, what would it look like, how would it feel for you, your partner and your children? What would your children notice? Asking all these questions about our visions for family life is very powerful.

When we do this work it can make us feel vulnerable. We are exposing a lot of ourselves. It may involve bringing up painful memories.

Although it might be challenging work, it can move us to a different level of relationship with our children. The "why" of our parenting helps us to have a deeper understanding of our children and leads to stronger, more connected relationships.

My parenting moved from a place of frustration to a place where Fred said, "Mummy, you haven't shouted for three years."

When Fred articulated that feedback it helped me see how far we had come together. I hated raising my voice; it made me feel out of control. I desperately wanted us to listen to each other. So that was the value and belief system that I worked on. "I want to feel calm. I want to be listened to and my children to be heard. I want everyone in this family to be understood and have their needs met."

Once you have articulated your metaphor and developed a vision about what you would like your family life to look like, take notice when something happens that is consistent with that. Feedback is very important. This is an ongoing process and it needs lots of practice. It is like a muscle, which needs exercising. It is tempting to go to the gym and give up if you do not get the results you want or expect after a couple of weeks, but giving up does not get long-term results. We need to stick with this. The ultimate result is to have an amazing relationship with our children. This approach needs to be practised daily – it's worth it!

Don't worry if you have a setback

As I said, it takes practice. Go easy on yourself. Even if you say and do something you regret, you are still on the right path if you know what your overall metaphor, values and beliefs are.

I feel guilty when I know I have not been calm, connected and conscious; however, I am a firm believer in working on being a better parent than I was the day before. Guilt isn't useful, so I get myself out of this state by asking myself: "How can I love my children more?"

End of the day reflection

At the end of each day reflect on something that has worked well. Focusing on this rather than on failure is more empowering and ultimately more useful in having a better relationship with our children.

There are days when as parents we feel things haven't gone well. We need to understand that we have done the best we could with the resources, energy levels and mindset we had at that particular time. There are moments when we are more vulnerable during the day. Something may have been said, or there may have been an incident that has upset us; then we are less likely to come up with a conscious response or phrase.

Ask yourself: "What have I learned" rather than striving for unobtainable parent perfection.

Children's feedback

I get my children to give me feedback just as I would give them feedback. I ask them, "What worked well today? Is there anything that I could have done that could have been better or made things easier?" They always give insightful feedback, and are always kind.

I am much more ready now to let go of my ego and say, "I am sorry I made a mistake" and I have noticed my children are now more able to say "sorry", too. I don't have to bark at them to say sorry - they say it because they feel genuinely sorry, rather than because I make them.

One of my motivators for creating The Why Parent was to say to my children, "I want to get better at being a parent". Articulating that to them was quite liberating. They have seen me read lots of parenting books and now they understand why.

Learning is a lifelong process and it does not stop when our children leave home. This is a lasting legacy of seeding, growing and nurturing the value of learning.

What is a good parent?

I ask for feedback now from my children on a regular basis. One day I felt brave enough to ask, "What is a good parent?" It is fascinating to get children's perspective of what they feel is a good parent. We were sitting at the dinner table and I thought, "Shall I ask this question or shall I just duck out of it?"

It was a powerful question to ask. Fred answered, "A good parent is somebody that always tells the truth and is honest." He also added, "and chooses a good nursery and good schools that are honest and truthful." It was interesting to hear that level of perception at the age of six.

Asking Tom the same question he said, "A good parent is somebody who tickles." I was fascinated to feel the difference in response to a fundamental question. Each articulated needing different approaches.

This also illuminated something else. I had always treated them in the same way and expected the same response from them. Hearing their answers and realising they needed fundamentally different things, it then made perfect sense that they were frustrated at being treated the same.

It is always a useful process to get feedback about what we are doing and why we are doing it.

Asking our children the question, "What is a good parent?" can be a good starting point for thinking about what we are doing well and those areas that we need to work on.

Activity

Ask your children, "What is a good parent?" Note their answers and your insights here.

Getting children involved

It is very powerful to get our children involved in thinking about how we work together. If we are doing something that might not be helpful as parents they can help us with how to do a better job. Or equally, if we are doing a good job we need to know what we are doing that works well, so we can do more of it.

What is actually going on?

The boys had been back at school for a couple of days after the summer holiday and after school they seemed quite boisterous and noisy with lots of energy. They needed to be outside and were being more physical with each other than they had been during the summer holidays.

I could have just ignored it and put it down to them having started school again, but instead I said to them, "I'm really not enjoying this. It looks like you are getting frustrated with each other, what do you think is happening?"

Tom answered, "I'm not enjoying it, too. It feels like you're telling us what to do."

This was interesting because I had consciously made an effort to not give lots of instructions, since they were just getting back to school routines after a long holiday of more choice and freedom; it was an amazing nugget of feedback.

I could have taken this personally, as a judgement of my parenting, but instead I chose to perceive it as an opportunity for the boys to express what was going on for them. I asked, "What is going to help?"

Tom said, "We need to be more polite to each other."

Fred said, "We are bossing each other around and being a bit rude."

It is a bit like customer care, asking the question, "How can I help?"

As parents we are sometimes scared of the answers we might get back, but we can really learn a lot. Children are likely to be noticing the same things we are, although they might articulate them in a different way. I encourage you to be brave and ask the questions, "What are you noticing?" and "What is going to help?"

Honesty is a great value to model to our children, as is openness to feedback; and getting feedback from our children is a really useful way of learning in our parenting journey.

Finding solutions to the current challenge

Sometimes the challenges of parenting can seem overwhelming. A process known as Solution Focused Brief Therapy (Steve de Shazer) is a useful tool, as it encourages us to articulate our ideal solution, to see past the problem, to a vision of what we would like things to look like if the problem was no longer a problem.

If a miracle happened and this issue was solved, how would life look? For example if mealtimes are chaotic and more food goes on the floor than in the child's mouth what would it look like if mealtimes were calmer?

Activity: Ideal solution

Think of something that is currently an issue for you. Now answer this question: If a miracle happened and this issue was solved, how would life look?

Now let's think about small improvements. Start by looking at where you are now. Using a rating scale of 1 to 10 (with 10 being the best it could be) give it a rating.

Current rating for this issue _____

Now, think about what makes it that rating? What is working to give it that score?

Now think about how you could move it one higher. What would that look like? For this it helps to think about the inner strengths and resources you have as a parent already. Focus on the positive aspects of what you do as a parent, notice those moments that are working well. How could you use those strengths to improve this issue?

What would it look like if it was one higher? What would our children notice if it was one better? What would your partner or friend notice?

What is good enough?

====================

Focusing on our strengths makes us more creative. Blame and guilt do not help us solve problems because we are in the fear-based brainstem part of the brain rather than the problem-solving prefrontal cortex. If we focus on what we do not want, we get more of the things we do not want.

Thinking about how we can improve things just one step on our rating scale empowers us to reflect on what we are doing that can help us move a step closer to our aim. We do not have to strive for perfection and be a ten. It is ok to be good enough.

When I ask the question, "What number on the scale would be good enough?" very often parents pick a six, seven or an eight. I have found that when parents are given permission to be "good enough" and not "perfect" their connection and love for their children increases and feelings of fear and guilt diminish.

Remember to refer back to why you are doing what you are doing. There is so much information out there in the media telling us what to do and how to do it. What I have found helpful is to focus instead on the "why". Having that vision, being good enough and noticing when things are going well helps us understand our values and what is truly important to meet the needs of our children.

Reflection:

"When we know ourselves in an open and self-supportive way, we take the first step in the process that encourages our children to know themselves."

Daniel Siegel

Activity

Give yourself a "you" rating from 1 to 10 – how true are you to yourself, how well does your parenting reflect who you are and what is important to you?

My "you" rating _____

What would raising the rating by just one look like? What would your partner, children, friend notice if you were one higher?

CHAPTER FIVE

POSITIVE LANGUAGE

"When words are kind and true, they can change our world."

Buddha

The fourth essential element of having an amazing relationship with our children is being positive. The vehicle for this is having positive language.

Why is using positive language so important for our children? There is a reciprocal relationship between our thinking and the language we use. Thinking unlocks language, and language is the key to our learning. If as parents we have positive thoughts and use positive language, then that really helps us to be role models for supporting our children to develop positive thinking.

If we use positive language it is less stressful for our whole body. Having positive thoughts and talking in a positive way releases more endorphins and oxytocin.

An everyday example of how this works, or doesn't, is if we are in a shop and the sales assistant talks to us in an offhand or dismissive way then we may put up resistance and are less likely to buy. If the shop assistant connects with us in some way, perhaps by having a genuine conversation about our day, then finds out what we need and shows us what the shop has to meet those needs, then we are more likely to want to buy.

Using a crude analogy, parenting is a bit like marketing: we need to find out what our children "want" and provide them with what they "need." We almost have to market thoughts, ideas and use persuasion in the process of keeping our children safe, helping them learn from their experiences and be the best they can be.

Encouraging a problem-solving approach

If we use positive language it eliminates a judgemental way of thinking. When we use negative language such as, "Stop doing that", "No," and

"Don't do this," this releases stress chemicals in the brain and children are in the brainstem rather than thinking in the prefrontal cortex. We are judging our children instead of seeing those moments as learning opportunities to help them problem-solve when they meet a similar situation again. We often expect our children to do what they "should" do from an adult perspective. If they are doing something that is inappropriate, we can talk to them in a way that helps them make sense of the situation.

In the summer, when we were at the beach, I saw a child knock over a cup of coffee which, in truth, the parent looked as though they really needed! The parent's immediate response was, "What's wrong with you? Can't you watch what you're doing?"

It is really frustrating to have a coffee that we desperately need spilt in front of us, but I am not sure we would say "What's wrong with you?" to a work colleague if this happened in a meeting. Why is it we use this language with our children? What belief does the child take away from a situation like this?

How does the child feel?

Putting myself in the child's position, I can see that if somebody asks, "What's wrong with you?" I might respond by saying to myself, "Is there something wrong with me?" "I always get it wrong", "I am not capable."

A more compassionate approach would be to empathise with the situation, to get them to help tidy up the spill and ask them what they could do differently next time. This helps them to believe that it is ok to make mistakes and that problems can be solved, rather than believing 'they' are the problem.

Being conscious of our energy

We need to be conscious about the energy we project in our relationships between parent and child. Whether it is at home or in school, children pick up the energy states of adults. In many situations, children experience predominantly negative energy in being told what to do and how to do it: "Stop this", "Don't do that." It would be great if we could turn that around and be more positive, reframing our language of "stop" and "don't", to the more compassionate and positive energy of, "What can we do to solve this?" and "How can we learn from this?"

Having a lifelong-learning, problem-solving approach ultimately supports a more positive and optimistic approach to life.

Every moment with our children is a gift when we accept them unconditionally for who they are, as they are.

Using positive language

It is important that we really monitor our language and think about what is the most powerful phrase or word that we can use in the moment. Our immediate reaction may be to say, "Stop it" or "Don't do it." If we are calm, connected and really conscious about what we are thinking and feeling, then we can come up with a more positive response. It also helps to have a bank of positive phrases to use.

Negative Language comes from feelings of:	Positive Language comes from feelings of:
Anger	Peace
Fear	Joy
Guilt	Love
Shame	Acceptance

Disempowering phrases to avoid using with our children

If you have any of the following phrases in your repertoire, think about what you might be able to say instead that is more positive – the second list will help with this.

- How many times have I told you?
- What is wrong with you?
- How stupid is that?
- What am I going to do with you?

- You always answer back.

- You never listen.

- Stop it!

- I expect more from you.

- You should know better.

- I can't trust you to do anything right.

- Look at me when I am talking to you.

- Stop yelling!

- Finish your homework now.

- You always leave things.

- Your brother never forgets anything.

Empowering phrases to use with our children

- Tell me what you need.

- I'm wondering ...

- I've noticed that ...

- It seems that you might be feeling ... is that right?

- Can I ask you something? Is this a good time to talk?

- How can we tell each other what we need?

- You seem to feel really strongly about this?

- What did you do to help?
- I can see that you might have that opinion. What else do you think happened?
- What would make this easier?
- What can we do to work this out together?
- What else? ... What else?

Disempowering questions

We can get bogged down with the practical aspects of parenting, particularly when we are short of time. When we are rushing around, we are focusing on what has to be done rather than on the qualities we want to encourage.

I am as guilty as the next parent of resorting to disempowering questions such as:

- Why do you always do that?
- Did you tidy your room?
- Have you finished your homework?
- What is your problem?
- Why do you keep doing that?
- What is wrong with you?

- Why aren't you ready yet?

These questions feel closed and judgmental. It would be hard to feel motivated and positive after being asked questions like these.

Positive recognition

Children need to be recognized for the things they are doing well. They need support for their efforts, improvement and the process, not just the outcome. Asking process questions, rather than result-based questions helps with this, questions such as:

- How did you know how to do that?
- I noticed you did that all by yourself.
- I can see how much effort you put into that.
- How did you solve the problem?
- What helped you get on so well with your brother / sister?
- How did you come up with that idea?

It is strange how as parents we spend more time thinking about what things to buy our children, than what language we use with them. The words we use with our children stay with them forever – the things we buy are usually temporary. I am sure you can think back to something that was said to you by teachers, parents and friends that has become a strong memory or story.

Our words become beliefs and our beliefs become values so we need to make them empowering and eliminate shame and guilt.

Reducing stress through language

Positive language is less stressful. Talking in a negative way heightens our state of alert and children pick up on that negativity. It ultimately affects our thinking and our emotional and physical wellbeing.

If we use positive language and reflect a positive belief system then our thoughts, feelings and behaviour are positive.

Go back to your parenting metaphor

Our metaphor for parenting and our belief system are reflected in the language we use. If our parenting metaphor is that "Parenting is a battle," or "I'm in charge" then our language is going to reflect that metaphor, with phrases such as: "Stop doing that", "Why on earth did you do that?" "What were you thinking?" "Don't do that", "Listen to me" or "What's wrong with you?" We can become wrapped up in negative language. "How many times have I got to tell you …?" and the classic "STOP SHOUTING," when we are in the heightened state of alert.

There is irony in telling our children to stop shouting at the same time we are yelling at them!

Our language is a reflection of our thinking. If we reframe our thinking from a negative, angry thought to a positive one, then our language will follow. We can turn it around quite quickly so we are not in that stressful, "Stop shouting" moment.

In that moment when our children are shouting, ask yourself, "What do they need?" Instinct tells me that when our children shout, it is because they do not feel listened to, understood or valued. We therefore need to use language that helps our children feel valued, listened to and ultimately understood.

Once we start asking that question of what do they need, then the thinking and language becomes a lot clearer. If we switch our thinking from "I am in charge" or, "Parenting is a battle or a test" to, "Parenting is a journey, or an adventure, or a gift to be discovered," then our language becomes much more positive. Our belief system and value system are instantaneously transformed and we make that conscious choice to think in a more positive way. So our language will naturally reflect more positive thinking.

We can then start reflecting on solving the problem, instead of, "What's wrong with you?" or, "Why did you do that?" We could think instead, "Well it looks like we have a bit of a mess. What do we need to do to tidy it up?" We need to focus on thinking more consciously about those phrases to empower our children rather than shaming or judging them.

It isn't always easy to be positive, especially when we are in a hurry or have a tight schedule and are thinking about what is coming next instead of seeing what is in front of us. It is an art that needs practice to say the most conscious phrase in that moment.

Activity:

Think of a recent situation where things didn't go well, where perhaps you said some things you're not proud of. Now on reflection, think of what you could have done differently. How could you have related to your child more positively? What could you have said that would have made a positive difference?

Situation:

What I could have said and done differently:

Some parents have argued that using a more conscious approach takes more time to talk and reason with our children. Although it might feel counterintuitive, taking some time to listen and talk through a situation resolves things much more quickly; our children ultimately trust us more and are more cooperative, which makes things easier in the future. Being listened to and having their needs acknowledged helps the child feel valued and understood rather than judged and unheard.

Understanding what is actually going on

One morning the boys wanted to play football in the garden before school. They had been playing a little while when I went out and said we needed to start thinking about getting ready for school. At this, Tom burst into tears. I could have rushed him through the crying and become frustrated by his reaction. Instead I chose to ask what he needed and he said, "I have not been in goal yet."

We talked about what would be a way that we could work as a team to get ready for school. The boys came up with the idea that Tom could be in goal first when they got back from school and they both felt it was resolved. If I had just said, "Come on we are going," regardless of the tears, my guess is it would have taken longer for us to get ready and out the door.

Using a calm, connected and conscious approach, asking that very simple question, "What is it that you are needing right now?" can save time in the long run as it helps our children to solve problems themselves. Throwing it back to them and asking, "What do you need?" or "What would help?" clarifies what our children are thinking and feeling.

Being the commentator

Our role can be as commentator for the situation: "I've noticed getting ready in the morning seems to be a bit of a problem. What can we do so that we are all ready to leave on time?" This type of questioning helps to open up the situation and is the start of co-creating a solution. It expresses the belief that we can work together to find a solution rather than blaming and judging.

The language is more positive and reflects the metaphor that parenting is a gift and that our children are here to teach us something. We learn from each other and have shared responsibility within the family. It is much easier to open it up to a problem-solving approach if we acknowledge each family member as equally valued; then we can solve problems collaboratively.

Being a curious scientist

Noticing what our children are doing, spotting the positives and really anchoring on to those moments help us to stay optimistic. Sometimes we tend to judge our children's actions instead of trying to really understand them. We pounce on those little details that you maybe would not with a friend. If we are in a restaurant with a colleague, relative or friend we would not necessarily focus on those little things: how they are sitting, point out their annoying habits or tell them to eat up everything on their plate!

With children we tend to magnify what they are doing "wrong" when actually there is a lot of what they are doing which is positive if we choose to notice. It is like being a curious scientist and wondering why our children are doing what they are doing.

It may be that our children have tidied their room and we focus on the one little thing that is out of place instead of noticing and praising their efforts. If we choose to focus on those little things that annoy us it is almost always a reflection of ourselves – those things that irritate us about our children often are the things that annoy us about ourselves. Be a curious scientist and say to yourself, "I wonder why I am so irritated at the way they sit at the dinner table."

Our children's value system may be different from ours

For a child, being in control of space such as their bedroom is symbolic of independence and we need to accept that our child's value system of cleaning the room may be different from ours. Telling an adolescent to, "Tidy your room now," when their values are focused on music, fashion and social media may not be as effective as opening up a discussion and working collaboratively to solve the problem. What might be an issue for you might not be a problem for them.

If we talk about the impact of what they are doing and how we feel about it, and that we are happy to work things out together, brings us much closer to a solution. Also our children are more likely to come to us about the things that bother them, which gives us the opportunity to know what their beliefs and values are, too.

Providing a commentary of what you feel is happening and asking questions about what support they need helps to generate a collaborative approach with a tone of mutual respect, rather than a battle of egos.

Activity: time to be brave

Think of an issue you have been facing with your child or teenager. Take a moment to describe the situation. What is actually happening? How do you feel about it? Take their perspective for a moment: what do you think it feels like to them?

When you are ready, go to them and have a discussion about it, and ask if you can work on a solution together. Take the role of commentator, and ask for their help.

Whose responsibility is it?

Some parents feel that is it their responsibility to make sure that tasks are carried out in the way that their values would dictate. They feel that they should be in control at all times and see any behaviour which shows the parent to be out of control as the child being insubordinate or disrespectful. If our parenting metaphor is, "I am the boss" or "Captain of the ship," the message is all about children behaving in an expected way.

Research about leadership suggests that strong leaders open problems out for discussion, delegate, notice positive action and spot what needs to be done. Effective leaders manage in a way that makes their team feel empowered.

If we are simply instructed to do something, it can feel disempowering and leave us feeling undervalued. Telling someone what to do is not strategic and does not help solve a problem the next time we might be in that situation.

For example, if we tell our children to tidy their room that is effective if we just want them to comply in the short-term at that particular moment; barking orders may not help in the long term, however, or empower our children to act independently so that in time they might not need to be told.

If they themselves see the need to tidy the room rather than being directed, they will also see the value in doing it.

Children want to contribute

Children want to contribute, be loved unconditionally valued, and listened to. When we ask them for their opinions and get them to solve problems, they are capable of coming up with amazingly creative solutions.

Ask them, "What can we do differently? What do we need to do to solve the problem?"

Asking questions empowers our children to ask those questions of themselves. Later down the line they are more able to use a problem-solving approach themselves, as opposed to the adult always having to solve the problem for them.

Activity

Ask yourself: What could my children do independently rather than me providing the answer? Think through their day-to-day lives and see where they could usefully become more independent.

Children are capable of understanding and using sophisticated language

Often we tend to simplify our own language when we speak to our children. We can underestimate our children's use of language. Building on the language that they use is really important. Children do not naturally use the language of, "Stop it", "What is wrong with you?" "What am I going to do with you?" "Stop answering back."

Children pick up the language used by adults, but in general children have a much more positive approach to life.

Processing positive language

It takes twice as long for the brain to process negative language compared to positive language. Using positive language with our children maximises their understanding of what we are saying.

As parents we sometimes unknowingly feed a diet of negative language to our children. We need to stand back, reflect on and analyse our language and our children's language and really focus on what we are saying.

Notice those moments when you have used positive language and observe how your children engage and cooperate; these moments are powerful to build on.

Language in schools

Looking at how language is used in school is really interesting. As a teacher and an educational psychologist I have had the privilege of visiting hundreds of schools. I have been more acutely aware of the language used in schools since my own children started their educational journey.

I personally find it uncomfortable when children are in situations where they are exposed to negative language and might pick up negative messages and belief systems. It is the implicit language that children absorb which impacts on the subconscious. If someone tells them they are not meeting "expected levels" in reading, this can lead to a whole range of beliefs about achievement, self-worth and being capable.

Results vs. the process of learning

Depending on the ethos and values of the school and the language that is used, children may pick up the message that results are more important than the process of learning. When I consult with children in school they now often seem to perceive themselves to be a number in the National Curriculum, such as, "I am a level two" or, "I'm working towards a level five."

This perception of being a number is counterproductive for having a lifelong-learning mentality. It becomes challenging if the values and language at home – which may emphasise creative thinking, lifelong learning and enjoying the process – clash with the perception of learning as a result reflected in a number or national curriculum level.

To me, it seems that the mantra and language in the education system is that if we are not able to measure the outcome then learning is not real.

With the emphasis on a National Curriculum, education has become driven by achievement rather than helping our children love learning. My view is that the overall aim of school should be to help our children enjoy their educational journey.

Successful schools emphasise positive language about effort, motivation, risk-taking and creativity rather than the end result. Tension results when the values of education and language in the home are different from the values and language operating at school.

Talk to your school

I encourage a shared dialogue between home and school regarding what you as a parent want for your child in terms of beliefs and values. In my experience, effective schools are those where there are opportunities to share values, beliefs and the language around learning between parents and school staff. If this is not in place at your children's school it may be that you can start the ball rolling. You might like to begin by giving a copy of this book to your child's teacher.

It is interesting that there is a political push for education to go back to a traditional exam system. In fact, industries are looking for innovative thinkers, entrepreneurs, and creative people who are able to cope with challenge and change. The predominant language used around education indicates that exam results are our ultimate goal as a society, when what we really need are innovators, creators, problem-solvers, risk-takers and communicators. Language in schools need to reflects this ultimate goal of industry, communities and society as a whole.

Go against the trend

What I see happening is that parents are latching onto National Curriculum levels and results as the focus, rather than asking the question: "What does my child need in order to be happy, to fulfil their purpose and to be successful in a changing society?" "What will equip them for the future?"

We need to understand the qualities, skills and experiences our children require to help them in life, and this needs to be mirrored in education. The very narrow view that ten "A –star" grades is the holy grail of the education system leads to children feeling guilt, shame and disappointment when they do not meet expected grades – they feel they are not good enough, when in fact they may have other amazing gifts and passions to give to the world.

The use of positive problem-solving language helps our children to become resilient and cope with challenges. We can help them learn to articulate the strengths and talents they have, that will help them reach their dreams, goals and potential.

What do you want for your child by the end of school?

When I ask this question, some parents say they want their child to do well academically but do not necessarily use the language of levels. Children do not instinctively say the words, "I'm a level four" – this language comes from the adults around them, which they model.

The majority of parents I meet say they want their children to be happy and healthy individuals; our job is to support our children to be who they need to be and this needs to be the focus in our schools, too.

When I ask parents what they want from a school, the comments revolve around having well rounded and confident children – this is in conflict with the government and Ofsted's, focus on results. Focusing on an arbitrary fixed outcome leads to a sense of failure if that outcome is not met.

It is always interesting talking to teachers who are also parents themselves. I find there is a tension between how teachers want to be – creative and process-driven – as opposed to how they feel they are expected to be, working to the constraints of the curriculum.

We need to get the priorities straight

We professionalise teaching through prioritising paperwork and administration, as opposed to really focusing on the quality of the dialogue and connections made between children and adults in schools.

My interest is on the quality of relationships in schools; this is reflected in listening, tuning in to our children and using positive language in schools. The notion of a good teacher for me is one who really takes time to listen, who values and understands our children.

When I ask children what makes a good teacher, the range of responses includes, "Someone who makes learning fun, lets us work with our friends, tells stories, lets us learn by playing games, listens to us, understands how I am learning." I have not had a child say, "One who gets me to a level five."

What are our schools teaching?

The school system is geared towards getting to the next stage of the education system, from infant school to junior school, from junior school to high school, from high school to university. It is also dictated by what universities want.

We miss where the child is right now and how we can develop their cognitive abilities at this moment in favour of thinking where they may be when they are sixteen or eighteen.

The current education system and the language in schools is very much top-down rather than bottom-up, and it is easy as parents to pick up and buy into the anxiety around getting our children to make the "expected level". We need to have the courage to meet their needs where they are now, equip them with the ability to learn, and trust them to manage the next level when they get there.

Reframing language

Making changes to our language can be a challenge. What we say and think is so much a part of who we are, an entrenched pattern from our values and beliefs. I always find it useful to be able to reflect and analyse our use of language with our children. For me, my goal is to get better at what I say and what I do with my children.

Active listening and positive language are the vehicles to have a better relationship with them. Start replacing habitual negative language, where it exists, with "curious scientist" language. This instantaneously transforms our thoughts.

The reframing challenge starts with thinking about what part of the situation might be difficult for our children and then asking direct questions.

Most people underestimate what children can do if we support them with positive problem-solving language. Preschool children are able to not only be cognitive about what they are thinking and feeling, but also metacognitive. Metacognition is the ability to learn about learning and articulate what strategies are being used when carrying out a cognitive task; for example, when reading, articulating: "I went back and checked that word because it did not make sense." Preschool children are able to articulate their thoughts and problem-solve if they are given the opportunity.

Being a calm leader not a behaviour-manager

Our children's language can become more strategic if we help them and give them the language of problem-solving. If we encourage them to start noticing what they are doing and how they are doing it, our children can begin to solve their own problems.

Using the language of, "Tell me what you need" and "I have noticed you seem a bit sad, what are you thinking?" "What would help?", "I am wondering what do you need to make it better?", "It seems that you are looking a bit frustrated and finding this tricky – what would help and make this easy for you?" helps them to think things out for themselves.

It is important to check out with them about what they are thinking and feeling rather than making judgements and assumptions about it. If as adults we were told we were feeling angry or sad or frustrated, we might find it judgemental and disempowering. Children feel the same way when we make assumptions about how they are feeling.

It is more respectful to say, "It looks like you might be a bit frustrated, is that right?" or "Would I be right in thinking that you're finding this a bit tricky?" This empowers them and facilitates their own thinking and feeling.

Language is a key to help them with their thinking, feelings and cognitive skills, and underpins the process of making sense of their experiences. Reframing language in a positive, respectful way helps our children give meaning to and clarify their experiences.

The stress of not meeting adult expectations

If our children are in a high state of alert their thoughts are in the brain stem; this inhibits imagination, creativity and the decision-making and reasoning part of the brain - the prefrontal cortex. If they are stuck in the brain stem they cannot solve the problem and understand what they might do next time.

Having an adult agenda and telling them what to do without explanation or choice keeps them in the brainstem. When we tell them to, "Get to bed", this prevents them from being able to solve the problem creatively.

Empowering children to make good decisions

One parent said that a more democratic approach does not work, "I have to tell them to clean their teeth because if they don't clean their teeth then their teeth will drop out."

I completely agree - there are certain situations where we have a responsibility for our children's health and safety. We also have to help them ultimately make their own decisions. There is a way of empowering children to brush their teeth willingly, rather than being directed.

If brushing your teeth is seen as a game such as, "How are we going to brush our teeth today? Are we going to brush as fast as a cheetah or as slow as a tortoise?" then children are engaged. We need to think creatively about the problem, not just tell them what to do and get angry when they don't do things the way we would do them.

It goes back to our parenting metaphor. If we are "the boss" we expect them to do what we tell them to do, when we tell them to do it, leading to a "battle," and feelings that there are "winners" and "losers." This ultimately leaves both parents and children feeling frustrated.

When we can let go of our ego and suspend our adult agenda to think about what our children really need, we all get a more satisfying result. Children need to feel they have some choice and control over the situation.

It is really important for both parents and children to be in that positive frame of mind which ultimately liberates us to be creative. We need to be clear and confident about our emotions, thinking and language so that we can be in an optimal positive state.

Sales

Gender is an interesting issue when it comes to my Why Parent groups. Often a woman will say, "I wish my partner or husband were here to understand this."

It was interesting working with David, who came to one of the parenting groups. His perspective illuminated a lot of the group's thinking and we went back to first principles. For him, his initial parenting metaphor was, "I'm the boss and they do what I'm telling them to do. If they don't do what I'm telling them to do, then that's disrespectful. I'm older than them, I'm wiser than them. They should naturally just do what I tell them to do."

It was great to have an open discussion about what children think and feel when being directed or told, and having their lives controlled, discussing the question, "What do children believe and conclude from that?"

David was feeling frustrated as a parent because he was not being listened to by his children and his children were not doing what he was telling them to do – feeling in control was important for him.

The children did not feel listened to because they were being told what to do all the time, without having an opportunity to respond.

The whole group benefited from challenging the metaphor of, "I'm the boss" over a period of time. It took two to three weeks for it to evolve. The moment of the shift in thinking came when we were talking about the possibilities of language and how we can reframe language so that instead of saying, "Stop it, don't do it. Why haven't you done it?" we can move to a more positive mindset.

As we were exploring positive language, David had his Aha! moment: "I used to be in sales and this was the kind of language we used in selling."

He then saw that we can use the language of sales with our children, not in a manipulative way, but in a way where we are almost selling an idea.

By week three, David's metaphor was, "As a family we work as a team and everyone has a personal best. We work together to meet our goals."

He shifted his thinking and metaphor from being a "boss" to being a "calm leader" and selling the idea of the family working collaboratively. David said, "I do not need to use the language of telling them what to do because we are all in it together to reach our goals."

Out of anyone in the group, he had made the greatest leap in his thinking. This highlighted the power of using our inner resources, using what we already know and focusing on our strengths to make parenting easier.

Conversely, just repeating what does not work over and over again reinforces the negative feeling that we are not a 'good parent.' If we reflect on our skills and strengths this helps to shift our thinking about parenting.

Not good enough?

There is a very powerful image I have that will stay with me forever. It is from the time when I first started teaching.

I taught in a little village school of just under 100 children and because of the numbers the model for the junior classes was team teaching, with several year groups being taught together.

I was in my early twenties, newly qualified and in the first few weeks of doing the job, and I was teaching with a very experienced teacher. In an incident that I will never forget, my colleague turned to an eight-year-old boy, picked up his work, tore it up and shouted at him, "It's not good enough. Do it again."

What struck me as a teacher, parent and just as a human being was to ask, "What are we teaching our children?" The message "not good enough" and publicly tearing up a piece of work in front of a child still fills me with sadness. What might that child believe about himself from the moment the teacher tore up his work in front of him?

What was even more disappointing about this moment was that the child had special educational needs and was extremely vulnerable in terms of his home life. What criteria made the work "not good enough?" I could see by his reaction that he was trying his hardest – for him it was his best effort.

This moment has always stayed with me in my professional capacity as a teacher, a psychologist as well as a parent. Why would an adult talk to an eight-year-old child this way? Was it to make him feel bad about himself? To make him believe he was not good enough?

It is really important that these messages are not part of school life and that we as parents we are not creating a belief that children are not capable.

Let's turn it around and ask what messages can we give our children in schools and at home so that they are not undermined, patronized, or made to feel small and controlled? How can we promote the message that children are central to their own destiny, able to make choices and decisions, rather than adults making arbitrary judgements about our children?

The experience has stayed with me as a powerful reminder. However frustrating or overwhelming a situation might be, I would never want to get to the point of destroying something a child has produced. When a child creates this becomes an inspired, precious and amazing act. Not something to be destroyed by an adult in order to fulfil the need to control.

Sometimes it is useful to experience challenges so we know what we do not want our children to experience. Having negative examples helps us to think about what we want to create for our children and what we want our children to believe about themselves.

Activity

What experiences do we want children to have? What do we want them to think, feel and believe as a result of their experiences? Think about this for a few minutes and write your thoughts here.

Negative adult beliefs and resulting child thoughts, feelings and behaviour

Belief	Thought	Feeling	Behaviour
Power is important	"I am controlled"	Anger	Aggression
Punishment	"I am insignificant"	Fear	Anxiety
Conditional love	"I am not capable"	Guilt	Give up
Disappointment	"I am not good enough"	Shame	Avoidance

Positive adult beliefs and resulting child thoughts, feelings and behaviour

Belief	Thought	Feeling	Behaviour
Unconditional love	"I am loved"	Love	Connection
Acknowledgement	"I am valued"	Value	Acceptance
Empathy and perspective taking	"I am understood"	Listened to	Understanding
Democratic co-creation	"I am needed"	Contribution	Cooperation

The Holy Grail of labels

Sometimes I meet with parents who want a quick fix for their child's behaviour and will use comments like, "He never shares" or, "She wants attention all the time", or "He is shy." Parents might say, "He always blames his brother and does not take responsibility for himself." As parents we sometimes want a magic wand to change our children.

It feels like some parents want me to have a sorting hat like in *Harry Potter,* to sort "Slytherin" from "Gryffindor." I have a problem with labels given by anyone other than the person who has been labelled. It is patronizing when someone else labels us – and that is how children feel, too.

Labelling is very restricting and judgemental. Once the label is given we are less likely to see exceptions.

Instead of thinking "never" or "always", look for exceptions to what your children are doing. Are we really noticing those times when our children are not doing that?

I remember a parent stating, "My child does not share." The work we did together was around the looking for exceptions. "Has there ever been a moment when he has shared?"

I could see the moment of realisation when she remembered occasions when he had shared. He had been sitting with his siblings at the dinner table, taking turns with paired reading with her at bedtime.

There is always a moment when, although it might feel that our children are not sharing, and sharing implicitly such as space.

It is very powerful to notice when children are doing well and explicitly point it out to them. There is a wonderful moment when we re-evaluate a situation, rethink it, reframe it in a positive way, and then challenge the truth of the statements we make. It is wonderful to see that shift in thinking and articulate, "Actually thinking about it, he does share. He did share a toy with his brother yesterday."

We begin to notice more of the things we want to see. As parents, sometimes we feel we have to label our children. Instead, if we choose, we can liberate them by noticing and accepting them for who they are.

Reflection

"Never speak out of anger, Never act out of fear, Never choose from impatience, But wait ... and peace will appear."

Guy Finley

Activity

How do you feel when someone describes you in a way that feels like a label or a judgement? (e.g. you never, or you always) Write your insights here.

As discussed through this chapter, we can use language that turns a challenging situation into a learning opportunity e.g.

What do you need?

How do you feel? / What are you thinking?

What have you learned?

What can we do differently next time?

Give yourself a "positive language" rating from 1 to 10 (with 10 being the best it could be)

My current positive language rating _____

What would raising the rating by just one look like? What would your partner, children, friend notice if you were one more?

CHAPTER SIX

ATTACHMENT

═══════════════════════════════════

"Being deeply loved by someone gives you strength, while loving someone deeply gives you courage."

Lao Tzu

The fifth essential element of The Why Parent process is attachment. Really tuning in to children is the key when developing amazing relationships with our children. That feeling of reciprocity between what our children are showing us and how we mirror and respond to that is so important. It not only helps the relationship we have with our children, it also supports them down the line in how they show up in their relationships with their friends, peers and in subsequent relationships with partners.

We are a role model for what our children believe about themselves and their relationships. If we put conditions on our relationship with our children they will mirror this in their relationships. When we use language such as, "When you have finished your homework you can watch television", why are we surprised when our children start being conditional with their friends and with us as parents?

Being mindful of our children's needs

Even when our children are *in vitro* we are more mindful than otherwise of what we eat, drink and experience. Before we meet them we are nurturing and connecting with them, playing them music, talking to them and feeling their movement and kicks inside the womb. These are all things that help us develop a dance of experience with our children before birth.

I remember the flow of Fred's movements when I was pregnant with him. There was a distinct pattern to the kicks and the punches. When he is asleep now I can picture the patterns of wriggles and movements of the elbows, arms and feet that I felt in vitro.

How we care for ourselves when we first know that we are having a child is symbolic of early attachment.

It is a symbiotic relationship. If we are treating our body well, we are treating our unborn baby well; it is an ecosystem of energy and emotion from the moment of conception.

Mirroring

After our children are born, that attachment continues as we mirror what they do as babies. It is an instinctive drive that we have as parents to copy what our babies show us from the moment we hold them in our arms. We love them unconditionally.

As our children grow older and acquire language, they start to develop their personalities and independence. When this happens, we may feel we have a loss of power. Our children are showing us that they are beginning to "find their feet" in the world, both metaphorically and literally, and we begin to feel that attachment weaken.

As toddlers our children start exploring, become independent and start saying "no." As parents we may see these actions as disempowering and a threat. The mirroring that was healthy before may mean we start to emulate their tantrums as we lose authority and control. We begin to get frustrated if our children don't do what we ask them to do. We lose some of that unconditional aspect of attachment we had when they were babies; we may forget to ask the question, "What do they need?"

What does this child need right now?

When I work in schools with parents and teachers, I ask: "What does this child really need right now?" I am a firm believer in continuing to ask this question whatever age our children may be.

With a baby their needs are immediate: food, a nappy change, more sleep, or to go out for a change of scenery and more stimulation. At this age it is instinctive to ask that simple question, "What do they need?"

As they get older it is hard to know exactly what it is that our children need all the time, but we can still make the best attempt at trying to match what they need with what we do and say; we can still tune in to their body language, eye contact or what they say. We can still engage with them and do our best to understand.

It is really important that we reflect on what they are showing us they want and need. Babies need to feel our presence physically. As children get older that physical distance increases but we know they still need to feel we are there; they still need to know they can say anything to us and it will not be judged. That original attachment and attunement is still fundamental to our relationship.

Feeling understood and valued

Attachment is a way to help our children feel that they are totally understood and valued, that their feelings and emotions are being read and tracked by us as parents; that there is total empathy, that we are truly present. It is like having someone walking beside you, but not necessary imposing their route or way of looking at the world. As parents, our job is to facilitate our children making their own choices, their own decisions and deriving their own meanings from the world.

With a positive attachment we help our children flourish and make the best of the opportunities that they experience. We don't impose our identity or our value system on them; we do not brand them as a particular individual. We enable them to make their own journey in the world.

Attachment is really important in helping our children find their own identity. They need familiarity, warmth and the presence of adults to give them a secure foundation to explore the world and make choices and mistakes in a safe environment. As parents our challenge is to allow that attachment to evolve throughout the developmental stages with our children. To do this we need to make choices based on the individual needs of each child.

Attachment needs

Some parents have an enmeshed relationship where they are dependent on the emotions of their children.

Other parents (sometimes the same ones) try to live their lives through their children and impose their values and way of looking at the world on them. This may come from a feeling of lost potential in their own lives, and wanting to give everything to their children in order that they can live the lives the parents wanted for themselves.

Other parents detach from having a relationship with their children because their own feelings and needs are not being understood and met.

We all have a different story to tell about our parenting style. Our own way of attaching and attuning with our children depends on our values about parenting coupled with our experiences of being parented ourselves when we were children.

From my own experience and in my work with parents and children there is a huge correlation between poor attachment and mental health issues of both parents and children. If a parent has a poor relationship with themselves, this impacts and influences a child's perception of themselves and the way they compare with their peers and others in society. Both parents and children can feel they are being judged.

Loving unconditionally

One thing we can do for our children is to not judge them, to accept and value them unconditionally. Sometimes we find that hard to do as parents because society conditions us to love conditionally. Loving unconditionally requires vulnerability. Like the Lao Tzu quote at the beginning of the chapter, it takes courage to open up, be vulnerable, and really love someone.

Our children are born with an indomitable spirit, energy and identity. I know there is a lot of research and debate about nature versus nurture, but from day one some babies are so alert and aware, it feels that they have seen the world before.

It is our job to let our children flourish without judging, without our own prejudices, and without our own values being imposed on them. We are here to facilitate our children finding their own way in the world, to help them see the world without labels.

The current system seems to compartmentalise people, and this is counterproductive to children reaching their potential. It is unhealthy to label our children. It impacts on self-esteem and is associated with anxiety and mental health issues.

Dependency on alcohol and drugs and risky behaviour start manifesting themselves when children do not feel they are valued, listened to or able to express themselves in ways that feel authentic to them. Poor child self-esteem comes about through adult judgement; children pick up from a very early age if they have been judged or labelled.

As an educational psychologist I see children being labelled as "naughty", diagnosed with "ADD," "ADHD", "dyslexia," and having "social communication needs"; I see children being excluded even at reception age. These are powerful messages we are sending out to our children about how as a society we are connecting with our children when we withdraw our care at such an early age, just when they are trying to make sense of a confusing world.

When children hear, "That is so naughty/lazy/stupid" they automatically pick up on that language and label themselves as "naughty, lazy or stupid." Adult judgements are very powerful and it is difficult for children to challenge that image. It can then become a self-fulfilling prophecy and an embedded perception of themselves.

Notice, breathe, listen, let go, and love

Imagine you are an adolescent student at secondary school and are having difficulties in making relationships. Imagine you are having arguments and fallouts with your peer group at school and feel that you are being bullied.

Thinking back to when you were that age, what would you really want your parents, your family members and friends to say? How would you want to be supported?

My guess is that most of us would welcome empathy and acknowledgement of the situation without being judged, labelled, dismissed or undermined.

We can never know completely what our children are feeling and thinking because we are not them. However, we can be compassionate and really listen without telling them what to do. That total attunement with our child, that connection is key. We don't necessarily empathize with their exact situation but we can understand how they may be feeling and we can encourage them to articulate their thoughts and emotions.

Early development of attunement and connection

It is really important that this attunement, compassion and empathy are modelled in the first six months, but if the first six months were not a great time for you in terms of post-natal depression, medical difficulties or sleep deprivation, don't feel guilty.

Even after years of anticipation of being a parent I was not prepared for motherhood and felt overwhelmed. My physical attachment with my first child was not "textbook" (whatever that is) compared to the immediate physical attachment that I experienced with Tom.

Feeling guilty about not meeting the expected "norms" of parenting held me back in developing my own unique relationship with my children; guilt isn't healthy.

For me, parenting is about acknowledging and accepting our relationship with our children at every moment. Instead of feeling guilty, I now ask more empowering questions such as, "How can I love my children more?" "How can I connect with them more?" "How can I be more compassionate and empathetic?" "How can I listen better to what they have to say?"

Another chance ...

There is another wave of brain development and attachment possibilities that happens in the adolescent years. It starts around ten to eleven years of age. Ironically, this is the time that our children are thrust into the complexity of secondary school life. Attachments at this age can be quite tricky because they are in a bigger community with more people to get to know. It is possibly the worst time to move to secondary school, with these big neurological changes and the onset of adolescence.

This second phase of brain development is a second window of opportunity to meet our children's attachment needs. The same principles apply: we can ask our children what they are thinking and feeling and be there to understand what they might be going through.

Simply thinking about how it would feel to be in that situation helps us to develop connections with our teenagers. Instead of blaming or judging, just being able to accept that our children might make mistakes is enough to help both children and parents feel more liberated.

Learning from mistakes

Making mistakes is a good thing; mistakes help our children on their lifelong learning journey. It is more helpful to let our children make mistakes when they are in our care, with our guidance, than when they leave home and are more vulnerable.

What we learn and take away from making mistakes is the most important thing. Risky behaviour is part of normal development for adolescent children. As a psychologist I would be worried if children did not demonstrate some testing and experimental behaviour. Sometimes people delay that until they are into their thirties and forties instead of doing it at a time that may be more age appropriate, and when support is on hand.

As parents we may worry about what other parents think, and that we will be judged by our child's behaviour. We may feel that we might be the only one who feels a particular way about parenting. There are as many ways of parenting as there are children and parents on the planet; each child needs a different approach that is authentic to them and their parent, according to their individual needs at that moment.

Trust your own judgement

We may feel judged if we are a bit more creative or liberal in our parenting than the next parent. We may feel guilty if we come down hard on our children by providing restrictive boundaries. We can be guided by having an end goal relating to the qualities we feel our children may need to equip them to enjoy life, flourish and reach their potential. What skills and attributes will they need, to cope with the challenges that arise in life?

My end goal for my children is to equip them to be independent and make choices; to be confident, happy and healthy, and to feel good about being able to develop a relationship with themselves and other people. Ultimately the focus of my parenting is for my children to go out into the world to fulfil their dreams, whatever they may be.

With that as the end goal, that helps me focus on what I say and what I do with my children.

Having a clear aim in mind gives us clarity of purpose and meaning as parents. If somebody feels the need to judge my parenting approach as not being appropriate, then I would always go back to first principles. Parenting is about our relationship with our children; it's not our job to worry about another parent's perception of our approach.

There are so many unique ways of parenting because each child needs a different approach, just as each child makes sense of the world in very different ways.

Wide-ranging perspectives

There are so many wide-ranging perspectives, even if we just take the one issue of helping our children sleep. For another parent to judge our parenting is in reality a judgement of themselves.

Once we have clarity about our vision for our family, it is much easier to make choices about what to say and what to do with our children about specific issues such as sleep.

Reflecting on what we want

Our previous relationships – whether it is with our parents, friends or partners – can have a massive impact on the way we parent our children. It is important that we take time to reflect on who we are, on our values and beliefs, so that we can make active choices about how we connect with our children.

Activity:

What is your end goal for your children? What qualities do you want them to have? Write your thoughts here.

Coming back to you

As parents it is really important to think about how we connect with our own parenting story and ourselves. The quality of our relationship with ourselves has a big impact on how we parent our children.

I work with parents who want to have a clear understanding of themselves – not in terms of ego. It's about understanding themselves in order to give more fully to their children. They are naturally empathetic because they have gone through that journey.

If we have attachment with ourselves, that facilitates our attachment with other people and allows us to have meaningful connections with our children.

We need to give ourselves permission and time to work out our relationship with ourselves. Some people might think that it is self-indulgent to do this work and to spend time on self-development. I am an advocate for working on our relationship with ourselves and knowing ourselves better than we did the day before, because we are then in a better place to serve other people, including our children.

If we understand how to connect with ourselves, understand where our values are coming from, we become stronger leaders as parents – not in the authoritarian sense but in a calm, secure, nurturing way. We are able to ask the right questions of ourselves and of our children, use positive language, and connect more fully and openly.

Having clarity of thought helps our children make sense of everything around them, and they can only do that if we can do it. It is not selfish to do that reflective work and understand ourselves as people. I would say it is the key to being a better parent, to having an amazing relationship with our children.

Connecting with our children ultimately supports them to be the best that they can be in the communities they are growing up in; it helps them make choices about what they want to do with their lives.

Patient vs. present

It was really interesting working with Alison in one of my Why Parent groups. She was an amazing, strong woman, the parent of a two-year-old, and very perceptive about what was happening in her relationship with her boy, Josh. She described absorbing a lot of the energy from Josh, who was having frequent emotional outbursts. Josh was feeling frustrated and angry in lots of situations.

Alison presented as very calm, able to articulate the situation, very patient with the child in many situations, whether it was on a long car journey, in the supermarket or going out shopping. It seemed that Alison was soaking up a lot of Josh's frustration, thinking that being patient was the way to go.

She said, "I don't want to react. I don't want to tell him off. I don't want to do the wrong thing or say the wrong thing." Alison felt she was treading on eggshells waiting for the tantrum.

The one thing that Josh was saying to her when he was frustrated was, "You never listen to me."

Josh repeated, "You never listen," and that was their mantra; his source of the frustration was that he felt he was not being listened to.

Alison had been incredibly patient, soaking up all this negativity, anger and frustration but it seemed like although she was listening, really listening, she was not connecting with what was actually happening. Josh felt he was not being understood.

The difference came when Alison's language started to change. Instead of just soaking up the tantrums like a sponge, she started responding in a way that Josh began to feel that he was being understood. Her language focused on empathy: "I understand you might be frustrated. It looks like you are pretty angry. This is a big emotion you are feeling." Using that kind of empathetic language really helped. Alison then began to not only be empathetic, but started to take his perspective, get down to his level and really understand where that anger was coming from.

She asked Josh what he needed and he articulated that he missed his dad. His father was posted to

Afghanistan in the armed forces. Josh was trying to make sense of his father being away for work; his frustration was an understandable reaction to his dad being away from the family home. He needed his mother to understand this.

For Josh, the key was not just being patient but being present. To be present and understand why Josh was doing what he was doing was fundamental. That shift was very powerful.

This type of perspective-taking is crucial in any relationship.

The Why Parent work is about getting deeper, connecting and being present; asking the questions, "Why might they be doing that? What is their belief about themselves to behave in that way?"

In the case of Alison and Josh it was interesting to see that the movement from Josh believing, "You never listen" and for Alison to start thinking, "How can I help him feel understood" was fundamental in developing a stronger relationship. Following a couple of weeks of active listening and really tuning in to what Josh needed, the tantrums diminished. Josh began to ask for more hugs and show affection to Alison as she was demonstrating she was listening and understanding his needs.

Unconditional love

Unconditional love is the foundation of any relationship. It is the first principle I go back to when I reflect on my relationships. It always reminds me of what Tony Robbins, the personal development coach, suggests for when we have a negative feeling: that we ask a fundamental question, "Who do I love and who loves me?"

This question demands an instantaneous change of state and always transports me back to moments when I have been completely overcome with unconditional love.

Asking parents to retell the moments of unconditional love for their child always brings a sense of the happiness of that particular moment and of the complete joy of connecting with and understanding their child.

One parent, Sally, described a wonderful experience of being on top of a hill trying to fly a kite with her five-year-old boy, Luke, and failing miserably. Both Sally and Luke were becoming completely frustrated with their inability to make the kite fly, and then Luke said, "It doesn't matter. We can do it another time."

Sally recounted this moment with a great sense of humility at Luke's awareness and understanding. The unconditional love she felt for him helped her move from frustration to thinking, "It doesn't really matter about the kite. What really matters is the time that we spent together."

In an everyday moment of frustration such as being broken down in a car with boisterous kids in the back, instead of thinking, "I could be home by now rather than waiting for the recovery van", with a bit of creative thinking we can turn it around to being a moment of connection. Thinking back to those moments of unconditional love, we can use the vulnerability of the moment as a point of connection with our children.

If we can do this, we realise, "This is a time that I will always remember."

I remember back to the moment when I came out of the hospital with my first child, thinking, "I have ultimate responsibility for the physical and emotional wellbeing of another person. They have just let me out of the hospital with this child, he is looking up at me, is totally dependent on me."

That moment of unconditional love for that child, no matter what, is a beautiful moment to cherish and something to call on any time we need to reconnect.

Unconditional love is that moment when the kite does not fly, the conversation we have while waiting for the recovery van, that joy of really understanding our children and connecting with them better than we did the day before. If, as parents, we live without judgement, give with no expectation, and love unconditionally, we are giving a never-ending gift to our children.

Reflection

"*Listen earnestly to anything your child wants to tell you, no matter what. If you don't listen eagerly to the little stuff when they are little, they won't tell you the big stuff when they are big. Because to them all of it has always been big stuff.*"

Catherine M Wallace

Activity

Think of a positive characteristic that you really appreciate about your child – something that fills you with unconditional love and makes you feel joy when you think about it, feeling a greater attachment to your child. It may be a word, phrase, or image that reminds you of that positive characteristic of your child.

Focus on this aspect of your child as many times as you can within the day.

Reflect on the day and notice how that characteristic helped your relationship with your child. Write your insights here.

Give yourself an "attachment" rating from 1 to 10 (with 10 being the best it could be)

My current attachment rating _____

What would raising the rating by just one look like? What would your partner, children, friend notice if you were one more?

CHAPTER SEVEN
RESILIENCE

"A life spent making mistakes is not only more honourable, but more useful than a life spent doing nothing."

George Bernard Shaw

The sixth essential element of The Why Parent approach to having an amazing relationship with our children is resilience. Resilience is a major strength, a quality we need to have in order to cope with the everyday situations that we face. It is the ability to handle both moments of extreme challenge and of complete joy.

Supporting our children to become more resilient in any situation that they encounter enables them to be flexible in their thinking, promoting character, creativity and curiosity. Our children are going to come across difficulties and challenges at school, at home and in the community and they need to be able to deal with them. How do we help our children make choices about what to do in challenging situations?

Being a role model of resilience in any challenging situation demonstrates to children that it is okay to come up against difficulties. It helps our children know that it is possible To solve difficult situations so they can do that, too. How we work through a challenge is something that they will tune in to. Our children have the choice to think, "This is difficult and I am going to give up" or, "This is a challenge and I can work it out."

Bounce-back ability

We need the ability to bounce back if we come across a traumatic situation in life, or experience loss and bereavement; we need strategies to deal with the significant incidents that happen in our lives. Resilience is the ability to cope with anything that life throws at us.

How we cope with a situation emotionally and practically is a significant message that we can give to our children. It is part of life to have something devastating happen to us. How we cope with it adds to our growth. We can see it as a learning opportunity if we choose to perceive it as such.

I remember at school, friends who completed the Duke of Edinburgh course described it as "character building". This was a euphemism to say it is not something that they would have chosen to spend their weekends doing, however the challenge was something that they were learning from. The qualities they said they had gained were perseverance, persistence and the ability to cope with challenges when things were difficult.

My husband, Av, uses the phrase: "experience is something you get when you do not get what you wanted." Sometimes we do not get what we want but we can learn from the "experience".

Activity

Think of some times in your life when you faced a challenge, coped with it and learned from the experience. Write down your memories here.

Strategies for challenging situations

What are some of the strategies that we might model for children when they come up against something challenging in their life?

With the children and parents I work with the key to building resilience is the language we use, which impacts on our thoughts and beliefs. We have a choice in how we process information when we come across a very challenging situation.

If we think about the fight or flight brain stem response, we could react in a very angry way if something traumatic happens. Somebody may say something very hurtful and we could react in an impulsive way and say something hurtful back, mirroring fight or flight behaviour.

Alternatively, we could see this as a learning opportunity and choose to respond differently. We could empathise with the other person and ask questions about how they might be feeling in order to understand the need to say hurtful things.

When this works well, we can store the experience to recall next time, drawing on it as a resource. Or we might think of a time when we have said something hurtful, where someone has helped us. Linking our experiences to the past and associating a story to the situation involves the limbic or middle part of the brain and helps us make sense of what is happening to us.

A calm, connected and conscious response

We can also come at the situation in a more rational, logical and reasoning way, processing the hurtful comment in the pre-frontal cortex part of the brain. We can think of the hurtful comment situation as a problem-solving activity and react in a calm, connected and conscious way. We can empathise with the other person, asking, "Is there a way I can help you? Or what are you needing right now?"

We can either have a creative response to a challenging situation or a knee-jerk reaction to a difficult event. As before, our children emulate our behaviour. If we demonstrate an empathetic response, our children will see that a difficult situation can be a problem-solving activity and that we can develop strategies to solve any problem.

The old adage is that if you give someone a fish, you feed them for a day; if you teach somebody to fish, you feed them for a lifetime. Solving our children's problems for them may help them today; modelling problem-solving and resilience allows them to solve their own problems for life.

It is an amazing gift to give to our children to experience a learning opportunity, as opposed to just telling them what to do and how to feel about a particular challenging situation. In the process they are also learning about learning.

Spotting patterns

We can also help our children to spot patterns and see the wider scope of how to solve problems. The technical term is metacognition – not just helping our children develop cognitive skills but also encouraging them to learn about their learning and be more aware of the strategies they are using.

How do we help our children think strategically so that the choices they make now will help them learn in the future?

Making connections with situations our children have experienced previously will equip them with a problem solving approach to life. The language we use can help our children see a painful experience as being an opportunity. Asking, "What have we learned from this and how is it going to help us grow?" gives our children the ability to develop themselves, and to bounce back.

There has been a lot of research focusing on the mindset of successful people. Talented and successful people in any walk of life treat failure as an experience that they learn from just as much, if not more, than success.

If we choose it, failure can help us to move forward, rather than being a negative experience; we can choose not to be a victim of circumstances. The key is to look back and learn from what happened, rather than give in to self-pity.

Connecting the dots

Steve Jobs maintained that challenges are about making connections and having enough dots to join in order to come up with a creative solution to any problem. Failure and half-right attempts can create the dots that need to be joined.

If our children perceive their parents treating every situation as frustrating, anxiety-provoking and stressful, they pick up that energy that everything is stressful, and they become anxious.

If we can think differently and ask, "How can I make this easier? What would it take to solve the problem? What else is possible?" we get a very different result. The situation might be unfortunate or inconvenient but we need a mindset that it is something we can work through. If we think like this, those moments can help prompt a calm, connected and conscious approach with our children.

Involving the children in problem-solving

I consciously involve my eight- and nine-year-olds in the problem solving process when there is an issue or challenge. For example, asking questions like, "I have noticed there seems to be some arguing at bath times. What do you think we need to do to solve the problem?"

When I unpicked this I found out the boys did not like the arguing at bath times either and they came up with solutions such as taking turns, negotiating who gets in the bath first and suggesting their own routines.

It becomes a natural practice and is essentially delegation because we are not dealing with the problem by ourselves, but co-creating solutions with our children. We are opening it out for suggestions, being flexible in our thinking and open-minded in our parenting to use a more democratic process.

Obviously there are those health and safety moments when we have to make split-second decisions such as when a child is walking out into the middle of the road. In these situations as parents we may not have time to delegate and ask an open-ended question. But in everyday situations it is a liberating process to designate decision making to be the responsibility of the whole family.

Sharing responsibility

This does not mean relinquishing responsibility but having a shared ownership of the situation. It is a process of reflecting on the question, "What do we want from family life?" As a parent do we want to be always telling our children what to do, barking mundane instructions, or do we want parenting to be a more curious experience where our children are seeing life as being about making choices, having fun and being creative?

Talking through situations when we are in difficult circumstances will help our children cope with any problem; they come to believe wholeheartedly that "we can solve this."

A daily choice to be calm and connected

I make a conscious choice to be calm and connected. It is a practice that I do every day. I am becoming so aware of a calm, connected and conscious approach to parenting that I can almost feel which part of the brain my responses are coming from.

I am not saying I am perfect as a parent – far from it, with the usual sibling squabbles and parenting frustrations – but my goal is to have a better relationship with my children compared to the day before. Being aware of my responses and why they happen helps me develop a better understanding of what my children need.

Activity:

Keep a diary of your calm, connected and conscious moments. As with every change we choose to make in our behaviour, feedback is essential in developing new skills. I recommend taking a few moments at the end of each day to reflect on the moments, which have gone well. You might also wish to think of the moments, which haven't gone well, and think about what you would like to do next time in a similar situation. It is not about judgement, but rather about supporting yourself to learn new insights into yourself and your children.

Having a calm, connected and conscious approach becomes a way of life and also impacts on the relationships with other people outside the family. The practice is about empowering ourselves, to then empower our children. If we model calm, connected and conscious behaviour, that helps our children feel capable and have a positive belief about themselves. If we support our children by working with them, instead of imposing our agenda and rules on them, then that is something they copy and integrate into their own relationships.

Involving children in decisions

A recent counter-example to this was when I received a letter inviting Fred to a Maths workshop with other students from other local primary schools. It was seen as a privilege to be asked to go to the workshop and when he read it he said, "Oh, I have been 'done to'."

It was really interesting that he chose to use that language because I perceived it as a great opportunity to be part of a different experience out of school. From his perspective, however, it was the adults who had made this decision: "It will be good for him to go" as opposed to him choosing that as something he would like to do at a weekend.

As parents, we might perceive this as being ungrateful, but another possibility is to see this from the child's perspective of being "done to" by well-meaning adults.

I had this experience myself as a seven year old when I found myself in a hearing-impaired unit, which was part of my primary school. I suffered from severe ear infections from an early age and as a result I now experience hearing loss and tinnitus.

What was interesting was that the adults had decided I needed to spend some time in the hearing-impaired unit rather than being in my mainstream classroom. It made me feel like Jack Nicholson in One Flew Over the Cuckoo's Nest, not understanding why I was there and not being consulted about whether I wanted to go there.

This experience has made me acutely aware in my work as a psychologist that we really need to ask children what they need and want, and not make those assumptions from an adult's perspective.

The idea of working together as a team, as opposed to children "being done to" by adults, is so important. In our society, now more than ever, there is a feeling that we are being controlled, whether it is at a government level or in a work situation. There is a lot more pressure, a feeling of loss of control over our lives, yet, ironically, we have more choice than ever before in history.

Working together in a collaborative way

Talking to the children I work with in schools, they generally feel controlled by adults, rather than having the opportunity to work together cooperatively. My ideal would be that we work together in a collaborative way with children, and use language that reflects this.

It is hard when we are in a society where there is a lot of pressure to conform. There are times when it is difficult to be democratic with our children. We cannot always allow them to do things that they may want to do, such as stay up all night, or have unlimited screen time.

How we live our own lives

If we live a life that is obviously unhealthy and not conducive to effective thinking, that will impact on what our children choose to do. There are ways in which we can help our children make productive choices. If we are making useful choices ourselves, and our children see a successful model of a positive way to live, then they will be influenced by that.

I am not advocating parents having a free for all and chaos. If we have a vision of what we want our family life to be like, that clarity makes it easier to focus on what our children need. Using creative language around collaboration rather than mechanistic, functional and directive language helps to promote a sense of cooperation rather than compliance.

There are many different ways to get the same result and if we ask our children to regulate their amount of screen time, for example, there are various ways to come to that result – we don't have to "hand down" the decision.

If we go back to the metaphor of, "I am the boss" and everything being a unilateral decision, then our children begin to think, "Where did that decision come from? Why am I only allowed twenty minutes a day on the computer?" Another approach is to open issues up for discussion.

An example of this was during a school holiday when I asked the boys, "How do you want to use your time during the holiday? What do you want to aim for by the end of the holiday?" Their plans did include time on computers, and they were also capable of setting their own targets, articulating, "I want to get better at riding my bike. I want to get better at football. I want to get better on the computer" and they were able to list how they wanted to use their time quite easily.

As a family we talked about how we could balance the time that we had; they didn't ask for an unreasonable amount of time on the computer. Because they had set their own targets, and also limits, they were more able to stick to them. So when I said, "I notice that you are on the computer. How are you getting on with your target?" the conversation was not focused on the time but on the purpose of the activity and the reason they were on the computer. Our children are more likely to self regulate if we encourage them to set their own targets.

Children's goals

Our children become more able to say what else they need to do in order to meet their goals when they set those goals themselves, which they will do when they are given the opportunity. It makes parenting more liberating as our children become more involved in the conversations, decision-making and goal-setting processes, rather than following orders.

When I consult with children in my role as a psychologist I meet lots of children who feel they have not got any control over their lives; and as they get older, feel the need to regain control through risky behaviour, such as experimenting with drugs, sex and alcohol.

If children feel powerless, micromanaged and controlled, that can show up later in life when they seek opportunities for some kind of control. The need to control manifests in different ways. Children often feel so constricted that they communicate through extrinsic dependencies and experience self-esteem and poor mental health.

Start with small choices

Perhaps if children are allowed to make small choices such as what they wear, eat and how they structure their day, some of those bigger issues may not arise in the same way. If we help children make those choices and decisions, it helps them be resilient to cope with challenges. When we take choices away from them, children begin to conclude they are not capable or not good enough. They doubt themselves because they are dependent on being told what to do by somebody else.

Once I saw a five-year old boy in an Easter Egg Hunt who seemed overwhelmed by the freedom and choice. He was not able to just go off and look for eggs because he was so used to being told what to do, and how to do it. The experience of the hunt was too random and liberating; when he found an egg he asked, "Can I pick it up?"

This raised questions for me about how we are helping our children make choices in their lives. Making choices, exploring, being curious and being creative in our thinking is important in life in order to be healthy and resilient human beings.

If we open it out, ask questions, and make connections between what has happened in the past, what is happening now, and what will happen in the future, our children follow.

For example, think of a situation where everyone else in the family is getting ready for school and a child is insisting on finishing a Lego model they are making before going to school (a situation that has happened many times in our household). They may argue, say it is not fair, want to finish the model, and refuse to get ready.

We could give a directive response and tell them, "Come on, get ready, you have five minutes to do it and if you do not do it you will not watch television when you get back after school." These consequences are not linked to what is happening right now. What we say to our children needs to be a natural response to the situation.

How would we feel if we were doing something productive at work and were told to stop doing that and do something else, "You have five minutes to finish that, then I want you to write a report that needs to be on my desk by five o'clock. If it is not done, you will have no lunch break tomorrow." Obviously we would feel frustrated, annoyed and disempowered at being instructed to do something without explanation. We would ultimately resent having to do the task.

If we stop, connect and empathize with our child and say, "I understand you want to finish your model. It would be great to finish it. We need to be at school for nine so you can see your friends, so I guess we need to start getting ready. What do you think we need to do to get to school on time?"

Let the child know what you need

If our children state what they need and parents clearly communicate what they need, we are halfway to solving the problem. As Dorothea Brande put it "A problem clearly stated is half-solved."

When children are given an opportunity they will often come up with some fabulous suggestions such as, "I can finish the part I am doing and I will complete the rest tonight." Children generally want to please and do not want to make us late. Sometimes spending time explaining what we are doing and why we are doing it saves lots of time in the long run.

There are lots of ways around any problem. As adults, sometimes our ego gets in the way and we feel our children "should" solve a problem the way we would solve it, rather than finding their own way. If we open it up, question, be curious and want to understand how our children experience situations, it improves our relationships. Children genuinely respect being part of the process rather than being told what to do.

I empathise with that feeling of frustration if somebody is watching you, monitoring you and waiting to pounce on you if you make a mistake. When we micro-manage our children that is how it feels to them. If somebody is counting down with "3-2-1" and breathing on our neck, we are going to feel fear and anxiety and not achieve our potential.

It is not our child's intention to annoy us or provoke us

Our children have not been put on this planet to irritate us or frustrate us. We chose what to feel about the fact that they want to finish the Lego model. It is a creative, wonderful thing that they want to complete their model. How we choose to respond to the situation is the key to whether it is a positive or a negative. Our adult agenda often puts barriers in the way.

It may be hard for us as parents to give up what feels like control to our children if we have not experienced this process when we were parented. It can be difficult to give this opportunity to our children if we did not have this opportunity ourselves. Some parents make observations such as "I was told what to do and it did not do me any harm."

If we involve our children they will see us as being logical problem-solvers who can ask open questions and think through to a reasonable outcome. The process goes back to our vision or metaphor as a family. If our aim is, "We are working as a team" then we all have a responsibility to work it out. If one person wants to finish the Lego model then that has an impact on everybody else in the family being late. The work is getting our children to be involved in that process of decision-making.

Knowing your strengths

It can be hard for parents to talk about their own strengths and qualities. Very often a parent can readily talk about the qualities and strengths of their children but find it hard to say what they themselves are good at or what they have done well. It is important to do this, both for ourselves, and to allow our children to do the same.

It is often easier to acknowledge our strengths in a supportive group, or when someone else points it out to us. Talking about our strengths is a really useful exercise when looking for ways to overcome challenges we may be experiencing.

I remember undertaking this task in a Brief Solution course. The facilitator would not move on to the next exercise unless we could articulate at least thirty-two personal strengths and qualities. We started off in pairs, taking it in turns to articulate a personal strength. It was a struggle. The question we had to keep asking was, "And what else? And what else?" It was a difficult task, as we are not often asked what our strengths, qualities and achievements are.

Activity

I encourage you to reflect on your achievements. Step back and acknowledge all the qualities, strengths and resources that have got you to where you are now as a parent. Exploring your skills and strengths is a useful process. Ask yourself, "What else have I done? What else have I used? What other strengths and skills have helped me solve a problem? What abilities have I demonstrated as a parent? … What else?" Write a list of your strengths, talents and skills here:

Focusing on those positive qualities is really important because that helps us deal with the next time we are in a difficult situation: the tantrum, that difficult question our children ask that we find hard to answer. What strengths will help us there? Those are the strengths and the qualities that we need to really focus on.

If we can articulate our strengths, then again our children pick up on that energy; if we are positive about ourselves then this is mirrored in our relationship with our children, and their relationship with themselves.

We want to bring out the "yes" energy as opposed to the "no". If we focus on, "Yes, we can solve a problem" our children feel that they are able to cope with anything that comes their way.

The key to resilience

The key to resilience is the ability to say, "I am aware of how I am feeling about a difficult situation. I have used strategies and inner resources to deal with difficulties in the past and this is how I am going to deal with it now."

Questioning ourselves

Any situation where children are experiencing something hurtful may lead them to doubt and question themselves. We need to discover what they believe about themselves. Somebody might have said something or done something that has affected a child's confidence and self-esteem.

Go back to being calm, connected and conscious as a parent to support them. We can get so wrapped up in trying to protect and regulate our children's feelings. It is a natural instinct to want to stop them feeling upset. Instead we need to empathise and acknowledge that it is okay to have those big feelings.

How we empower our children to feel a painful emotion is important. Feeling emotions of being frightened, frustrated or angry that somebody might have hurt them is part of a learning process. We need to help them work through these feelings and emotions; this is crucial in developing their resilience.

Use stories of how they have coped in the past

Refer back to stories of how they have coped with difficult situations in the past; linking that to the challenges they are facing now helps them feel empowered, connected and able to understand their feelings. Remembering a situation where they may have been hurt previously and what they learned from it will help them think how to solve the problem now.

It is part of being human to have emotions of anger, frustration and guilt. I worry about those children I see in schools who do not show a range of emotions, who are mono-emotional. We can help our children perceive that solving a problem and coping with a difficult situation can be positive, even though it is painful. We need to help children verbalise their emotions and to empathise with the feelings of other people involved in the situation.

Seeing the other person's point of view

Imagining what something feels like from someone else's perspective shifts our children's thinking and enables them to connect with somebody else. Using phrases such as, "I am wondering how the other person might be feeling?" will help our children to see things from other points of view.

We can help our children cope with moments of anxiety, fear and frustration by using language of resolving conflict such as, "What would it take to solve the problem?" Our children are very capable of coming up with solutions if we give them the opportunity.

Resilience in victory and defeat

It was a great day when Fred said to me, "It is not about the trophy, it is about knowing you have done well." He also as an afterthought pronounced, "And it is not about the size of the trophy!"

For professional cricketers "The Ashes" is probably the smallest trophy you can win, but it also tells the biggest story. The history surrounding the ashes is huge in that it symbolises the battle between two great cricketing nations of England and Australia. I am not sure if it is the smallest trophy in sport, but the passion with which it is contested is immense.

For Fred, he was reflecting on winning a trophy in Tae Kwondo. He had got a bye into the second round and found himself in the quarter final of the British patterns competition without realising it. He nailed the sequence of the moves in the quarters and froze in the semis, but because he ended up in the semis he finished with a joint third place trophy.

The next event was the high kick, a discipline, which involves kicking a ball suspended from a pole. One by one the hopeful contestants aim their foot at what looks like a dangling tennis ball. Fred found himself in the final with a girl who looked three years his senior and who was several belt ranks higher. It did not help that the referee raised the tension by announcing it was "girls against boys" for the kick-off. It felt like the Karate Kid. Both kicked the first height and the second. They then both missed the third attempt and the referee reduced the height of the ball. It was tense. The result was that the girl kicked the ball fair and square and Fred missed his attempt. Fred came away with no trophy, as in this event only the winner won a trophy.

What was amazing was that afterwards Fred commented that the girl had deserved the win because before the kick-off she had said "good luck" to him, a great sporting gesture. Fred had remembered that the girl had achieved second place in the event last year. He was generous in defeat and genuinely learned something from the experience.

In the first event he had won a trophy and had not performed his best. In the second he had no trophy but gained the truth that it was not about the trophy, he knew he had done his best and not given up. It reminded me of the great movie quote from Rosie Perez in White Men Don't Jump: "Sometimes when you lose you really win."

Outcome thinking and rewards

Sometimes we pounce on something we see our children do well and praise the outcome. I see a lot of children coming home with stickers for sitting on the carpet nicely or for having eaten their lunch. These awards are for things I would expect children to achieve in the normal course of events in school without having to have an acknowledgement or a sticker. Getting a sticker for mundane tasks of conforming causes our children to conclude that being average gets praise and a reward from adults.

Extrinsic rewards are counterproductive to making real connections with our children. If adults model valuing external items such as stickers, marbles or pasta in a jar, children begin to value objects and rewards. We then wonder why children become focused on material items. Some schools have an online reward system for the pupils to collect points for iPods and other gadgets. If we want to connect with our children then we need to help them see life as a process and a gift to be enjoyed. Do we want children to believe that things are only worth doing if they are rewarded externally.

A connection with our children does not need to be validated with an object or extrinsic reward; connection is expressed in a hug, a smile, active listening or a kind word.

Effort, motivation and passion

What children need is for their effort, motivation and passion to be genuinely acknowledged; they need to be valued for their unique way of looking at the world. It is innovation, creativity and extraordinary thinking that need recognition, rather than sitting nicely on the carpet. Rewarding mediocrity and conformity does not lead to happy, motivated children.

What do we expect our children to conclude when adults say, "Well done" with a sticker? Celebrating "sitting nicely" gives the message that it is the "right choice" to be average and controlled.

Collaboration, perseverance, positive attitude

The qualities that society needs are collaboration, perseverance, positive attitude, and motivation and as adults we can model and acknowledge these traits for our children. If we want to create a society that is more forward thinking, imaginative and creative then giving stickers for lining up nicely is not the way to do that; it is not going to create the next great risk-taker, such as Steve Jobs, with Apple's philosophy of "think different".

Extrinsic rewards suppress creativity and freedom of expression, things our children naturally show us from day one.

Intrinsic rewards

A better focus is on intrinsic rewards, allowing children to value what they do without an adult needing to pass judgement. We can encourage our children to reflect on what they have done and how they feel about it. For example, instead of saying, "Well done, great job," we can say, "When I read your story it reminded me of .../it made me feel ..." or ask them, "What do you think about your story?" This then focuses on the impact of the work, connects it to a previous experience and also encourages our children to articulate what they think about their work, and not be dependent on adult judgement.

Time-out vs. connection

The experience of using "time-out" was the reason I wanted to change my approach as a parent. I have subsequently heard lots of parents say they want to change their approach from using rules, rewards and consequences. Implementing time-out was, for me, an inauthentic way of parenting. Use of this type of parenting strategy seems to be in opposition to a mutually respectful relationship.

The parents I work with instinctively know they want an alternative to the behaviourist model of manipulating and controlling their children, but they are not sure what to replace it with.

I attempted to use time-out with Tom, my youngest child, when he was three years old. It seemed I did not need to use any type of rules, rewards and consequences with Fred, as he seemed to naturally follow verbal explanations. If I provided a running commentary about what was happening or why something was happening, Fred appeared to understand.

At the time of the time-out, Tom was experiencing fluctuating hearing loss and was probably missing big chunks of instructions and information. Thinking it through later, what he needed was a more physical and visual approach to understanding what was happening.

I found myself one evening in a chaotic bath-time situation where the boys were getting very physical with each other. They were running around, pushing and shouting. It all felt very out of control.

For some reason, Tom was getting more and more frustrated and hit Fred. I felt that I had exhausted every strategy I had. With a heavy heart I physically *picked him up and put him on a 'time-out,' step. It was the least useful action that I could have taken for Tom at that particular moment in time. To this day, he mentions "the naughty step" even though it has been used on two occasions and was never referred to as such. In both situations he could not remember the reason why he had been forced to sit there.*

I felt I had lost a part of myself. Even just thinking that word – "lost" – makes me feel sad that I resorted to using an intrusive, ultimately ineffective strategy. My metaphor of parenting changed from that moment. I saw Tom crying and looking at me as if I had betrayed him. I had "lost" and with it I felt metaphorically lost in what to do and what to say. When I looked into his eyes, knowing the truth that he had no idea why he was sat there, I felt guilty that I had made him feel shame. I knew I needed to do something different.

A situation had arisen in which he felt frustrated and lashed out at Fred, but this was not the answer. In neither the short nor long-term had time-out helped Tom understand how he was feeling and why he had hit Fred. All it had achieved was to make him more frustrated. He was being isolated and I was withdrawing my love from him at the time when he was trying to understand a challenging situation.

Walking away and telling him that he had to think about what had just happened was a totally ineffective thing to do to a young child – particularly a child who was not understanding verbal instructions and information. For me, it was a defining moment that I keep revisiting. From that moment I knew that I wanted a more compassionate approach to parenting. Parenting for me now is not about winning and losing, it is about co-creating experiences.

Compassion and love vs. shame and guilt

Time-out, rules, rewards and consequences are not effective strategies for reaching our long-term aims for our young people. Shame and guilt are not the answers to parenting.

The antidote to this approach is compassion through love, joy and peace. I know now that my parenting failure was at least a move towards progress. My failure as a parent in that moment has helped me move on to want to be a better parent than I was in that bath-time moment.

Using fear, shame and guilt as parenting tools leads to unhappy parents and children. Although this has been a hard lesson to learn, it taught me so much about what not to do if we want happy children with strong self-esteem and confidence. Being vulnerable helped me experience a better connection with my children. Brené Brown writes in her book "Daring Greatly" that, "vulnerability is the catalyst for courage, compassion and connection."

Encouraging children to talk about emotions

As parents we need to encourage children to articulate what they need and how are they feeling; not to remove them from the situation unless that needs to happen for health or safety reasons.

The bottom line is how do we help our children feel safe? When a child is hitting another child, what is an effective way of dealing with it? Talking it through at that moment in time might not be the best way of handling something when emotions are high. Children might need to be separated; but there is a way of being authentic and respectful, rather than parenting from the energy of anger and shame, saying and doing things we might regret later.

I have talked to Tom about the experience of using time-out and I will continue to learn from it. I am hoping Tom knows that I am not that person now and that I do not ever want him to feel guilt or shame.

I now approach life in a different way, making more conscious choices and being calm and connected with what I say and do. It is that modelling I am hoping my children pick up.

If we use rules, rewards and consequences, children start to expect rules, rewards or consequences from an adult in every situation. They begin to expect an adult judgement on what they do, as opposed to being able to regulate their feelings themselves and understand what they need.

Using parenting approaches, which involve love, joy and compassion helps model what we need to see in our families and communities.

Reflection

"The mediocre teacher tells. The good teacher explains. The superior teacher demonstrates. The great teacher inspires."

William Arthur War

Activity

Think of a challenging issue you are experiencing at the moment with your child. How can you make it a co-creating, collaborative problem-solving response rather than a directive response?

Give yourself a "resilience" rating from 1 to 10 (with 10 being the best it could be)

My current resilience rating _____

What would raising the rating by one look like? What would you, your partner, children, friends notice if you were one more?

CHAPTER EIGHT

ENJOYMENT, NOW AND THANKS

"The reason people find it so hard to be happy is that they always see the past better than it was, the present worse than it is, and the future less resolved than it will be."

Marcel Pagnol

The last three essential elements of being a Why Parent are **Enjoyment**, living in the **Now** and giving **Thanks**.

Being calm, connected and conscious helps us to reduce stress and anxiety and helps us enjoy our children. I have worked through the process of The Why Parent with many parents, focusing on wellbeing, being positive and really connecting with our children. Sometimes it is hard to move forward in our lives and our parenting because we are still preoccupied with what happened to us in the past.

I certainly felt there was something stopping me being the parent I wanted to be. I was blaming something that happened in the past and I created a self-fulfilling prophecy, recreating the past with my own children and perpetuating a cycle of negativity. I knew that negative beliefs and self-sabotage had to stop, in order for me to enjoy my children.

We can choose to reinforce and recreate the parenting model we were given or we can reject it and follow a different path.

Very often there is a pattern to the way that we parent and we may have some neuroses about the past. We can also have anxieties about the future and project an image of what our children will turn out to be. Sometimes we see something in our children and make a huge extrapolation, "If he does not say 'please' and 'thank you' then everyone is going to think my child is rude and he will end up with no friends."

In mapping out their whole future in a "flash forward" of what we think they are going to be like, we start creating a mythology about the past and future. In the process we can miss what is right in front of us: our children being amazing.

The art of savouring every moment

It is a real art to be able to savour every single moment with our children. It is an art we have to practice. It is similar to going to the gym and working out a certain set of muscles; over time it becomes a unconscious act.

This practice, of using the muscle of the brain and heart, being in the "here and now" with our children can become a habit.

We might have our agenda, "I can't let them do that because my parents did not let me do that." Our preconceived ideas can get in the way: "I can not give them a hug when they are screaming because I will be rewarding their bad behaviour." Our ego and the past can get in the way of giving our children what they need.

We attach values to certain things that we do and it is important to explore where these values come from and why they have suddenly sprung up as an issue, so that we can make a conscious choice about whether to keep them or not.

Why is it so irritating when they flex their independence and answer us back? We need to know what our values are and what our children value so we can understand each other better. This then helps us focus on what is important in that moment, helps us enjoy the moment rather than judging our children for what they have done in the past or what we think they will do in the future.

Living in the now and focusing on what we are experiencing in the present is the only thing that we really have any control over – how we feel and think in that moment, and what our emotions are in that moment. The author and speaker Brendon Burchard asks the question "did I live, love and matter?" This is a great question to ask in order to live a life in the present and with purpose.

Truly feeling our emotions

Sometimes I think we do not allow ourselves to really feel our emotions because we are preoccupied with what has happened to us in the past or worried about what will happen in the future. We do not give ourselves permission and time to feel because we are too busy. We think about what might happen in the next five minutes, or the next half hour, or the next day, or the next five years. "Grown up thoughts," get in the way.

But we can't change the past and we can't control the future. All we can enjoy is the moment we are in right now and we do that by embracing our feelings and thoughts. Children can do that so brilliantly. They can enjoy the simplest pleasures in the moment of exploring mundane objects. As adults we lose the sense of fun and play. We question everything: "Why am I wasting time doing this when I could be doing all those things on my to-do list?"

In loving the moment we have to relearn the ability to enjoy simplicity instead of overcomplicating everything. We sometimes compartmentalise and label situations and people, making things more complex than they need to be. Going back to the simplistic enjoyment of the now is key to helping us connect with our children.

Time to ourselves

If you had some time just purely to yourself, how would you use it? It's not always easy to find, but it is important that we have some time to ourselves, to recharge and reconnect with ourselves. What would you do with it? What would it look like? What would it feel like?

Take a moment to get into that feeling of flow, enjoyment and pleasure, of just being – this is when you remember who you are.

We tend to stop recreating ourselves when we become parents.

Am I really shopping?

I remember the day Tom started school. Now both of my boys were on their educational journey. I ended up in a clothes shop. I do not know how I got there or why, as anyone who knows me is aware that shopping for clothes is not my thing. The predominant colour in my wardrobe is black following an eighties diet of indie and alternative music with the prerequisite "Goth" uniform.

I first wanted to know why, out of anything I could have chosen to do with the freedom of my children now in school, I found myself in a designer shop rifling through clothes. I simply had lost the art of how to shop. My experience of shopping with two boys had always been a window of opportunity of ten minutes, which meant buying the same type of underwear in Marks and Spencer for the last nine years because I knew where they were and could plan the route and exit like a finely tuned "Oceans 11 pre-school" heist.

What do you enjoy doing?

When we have children our identity can change out of all recognition and we do not know ourselves as being the person from a previous existence. In thinking about time for yourself, reflect on things you enjoyed doing, whatever it was, before children (BC) and after children (AC). Your interests may have changed and evolved into something different, but there are likely to be some elements that were there before.

Creating and enjoying that time again is fundamental to recapturing what makes us essentially who we are. It is wonderful finding out that regardless of all the changes, which have happened since having children, you are still you. Ask yourself, "What essentially makes the essence of me?"

Activity

═══════════════════════════

Plan some time on your own. What would you do? Where would you go? It may seem like a distant dream at the moment, so let yourself dream it ...

And now, think about where and how you could find that time ...

When I ask this question, the responses I get from parents are usually simple things like just having an uninterrupted cup of tea, reading a magazine; going for a walk, watching what they want to watch on television, or reading a novel - they are wide ranging responses, from physical and being outdoors to just being still and listening to ourselves.

Sometimes the response is, "Well, I don't have time to read." This in itself tells us a lot: perhaps it is time to make time for the things you need and enjoy.

Demonstrating development of skills

We are role models for our children. It's important that we spend time doing things we love and are good at, partly so that our children learn to do the same. They pick up on the fact that it is okay to really focus on something, to enjoy it in the moment and to give it our attention and concentration because that is how we become fluent.

Malcolm Gladwell reported in the popular book *Outliers* that we need to practice a task for at least 10,000 hours before we master it (based on the research of Dr Anders Ericsson). Children need to know that we have to concentrate and to focus on something to be successful at it, and that comes down to the element of enjoyment.

If we enjoy something we will want to practice more, get better at it and do it all the time, whether it is playing tennis, football, reading or playing the piano. If it is something we love doing we can be in that moment of living in the now, where five minutes doing something effortlessly turns into half an hour or an hour. If our children see us doing something that we really enjoy and are good at, that is an excellent model to have in life.

Appreciation

I love to ask the question, "What do you really appreciate about your child? What is a quality that your child has, that when you really think about it, makes you think they are amazing and makes you smile?" Articulating what you appreciate about your child or reflecting on an activity you enjoy doing together can help you to feel a connection with them.

Activity

Write down three things you appreciate about your child.

What is one quality your child has which you think is amazing?

What are some activities you enjoy doing together?

What is one memory you have about your child that – when you think about it – fills you with complete unconditional love?

Being present in the now

This last question is the most powerful question I have found to help parents connect with their child. The feelings of appreciation, enjoyment and love are overwhelming. The question brings the feeling of love and appreciation present into the current moment, and helps us enormously with living in the now.

This is the essence of a full, satisfying life: actually feeling the joy of things as they are happening.

One parent took a while to come up with an answer to the question and then said that that the moment was recreated every morning in bed with a family "snuggle."

This helped her realise that moment of unconditional love for her was the moment of birth, of holding her child for the first time. The parenting metaphor she then came up with was, "Giving birth every day". This moment was transformational in that she now had an image to help her connect more fully and openly with her children whenever she wanted and needed to.

Sometimes we overcomplicate and over-think things. When we can reduce our connection down to its simplest form we can then enjoy it easily. Life can be reduced down to choosing pain or pleasure.

Everything in life can be reduced down to those two experiences.

We also have a choice about how we view pain and pleasure. If we understand that life can be painful but also incredibly pleasurable if we enjoy the moment, then it makes it a lot easier to cherish every minute with our children. That shift in thinking has helped me, and the parents I work with in being more present.

Breathing

One way of becoming present in the moment is to be conscious of our breathing. The only things that we can be sure about in being alive are our breathing and our heartbeat. Even just putting our hand on our heart, feeling our heartbeat, or feeling the motion of our breath can help us slow down and connect with ourselves, and the present moment.

When we have more oxygen going to the brain we are more aware of our thinking, and this helps our decision-making and being in the now. Taking a few conscious breaths, deeper than usual, helps oxygenate the blood more fully.

I read The Power of Now *by Eckhart Tolle when we were stranded in Spain on holiday. There was not much we could do about it – it was Easter 2010 and an ash cloud from an Icelandic volcano was impacting on the skies of Europe, preventing aircraft taking off and landing. Thankfully it was a nice place to be stranded for a week and* The Power of Now *was the perfect book to read when feeling quite powerless.*

There was no internet connection where we were staying, so we could not book a rescheduled flight back. Eventually a group of fellow stranded holidaymakers decided to collectively problem-solve the situation and organised a coach back to England. The ash cloud was something that we could not control.

This helped me realise a basic truth: that you cannot control the past, you cannot control future events but you can enjoy the now; it meant an extra week in Spain, which was fabulous!

It is really useful as a parent to model "enjoying the now" with our children. We could have been cross that the insurance company was not going to pay for the additional costs of accommodation and return travel back home, but this would not have helped.

Instead, we reframed the situation: I perceived it as an adventure and an extended holiday with all the learning associated with a land and channel journey across Spain, France and England. Instead of being frustrated with the situation we made calm, connected and conscious decisions about what we said and what we did and modelled that for the boys.

Thanks

Research studies focusing on gratitude link this practice with greater states of happiness. The positive psychology work of Martin Seligman, Barbara Fredricksen and Carol Dweck has been instrumental over the last ten years in deepening our understanding of the neuroplasticity of the brain. We now know that we can make choices about how we feel and how we think, and this has an impact on what we believe about ourselves.

Gratitude is an integral part of our ability to consciously raise our happiness levels. People who give thanks and are grateful are more enthusiastic, more interested in life and generally happier.

Research is beginning to put figures on and measure happiness levels, but without having to put numbers on happiness, at an instinctive level we know that if we feel thankful, if we acknowledge what we have to be grateful for, we are also happier and more positive with our children. If there is more positive energy in the home it is going to create a calm and creative environment for our children to flourish.

Gratitude increases optimism

Gratitude increases our optimism, feelings of hopefulness, empathy and compassion. What greater skills, qualities and strengths do we want for our children than to be optimistic, compassionate and able to empathize with other people?

If we bark at our children to say "please" and "thank you", parrot fashion, then they will just be dependent on somebody telling them to say "please" and "thank you". But if we say "thank you" when someone does something for us, then our children will feel our gratitude and emulate the practice. I know it is very difficult to say "thank you" to a traffic warden as they are placing a ticket on your car but there are genuine moments when we can be thankful for unfortunate situations. We know that somewhere down the line (even though we do not know exactly how, at the time) we will have gained something from the experience.

Think of things you are grateful for, and help your children do the same. Even simple acts of thanks are very powerful. I help my children to do this at dinnertime or bedtime, depending on when it feels more likely they are in the right frame of mind to review their day. Sometimes it is dinnertime when they are chatty and on other occasions it is bedtime when they are winding down and reflecting about what has happened during the day.

E.L.T. time (Enjoyment, Learning and Thanks)

I encourage Fred and Tom to articulate three things: what they have enjoyed, **E**, what they have learned, **L**, and what they are thankful for, **T**. We call it our "**E.L.T.**" time. It supports them to think about something that a friend did or said to them, what happened in the playground or in class. This is a really powerful way to help our children celebrate what they have enjoyed, learned and are thankful for.

Activity

Try having some "ELT" time with your own children, and see how it goes. Write down what happens here.

It really helps to notice those positive moments and it is amazing how when we notice what children are doing well, they do it more. It is also really powerful to collect those moments, and celebrate them as a family; and to build the feeling of gratitude.

Savouring amazing experiences, whether it is in the park, weekend events or school holidays, builds a store of memories that you can then talk about as a family. These moments are powerful because they become the stories your children will remember; they become a part of family folklore. Sharing good news and memories from our experiences helps us to feel happier and more grateful.

Positively processing emotions and experiences

The memory and story element of this practice activates the middle part of the brain, the limbic system, where we make sense of all our emotions and experiences.

We are linking and connecting aspects of our lives all the time. Anthropologists believe that seventy percent of what we learn is through stories. We can help our children create their own life story by giving them opportunities to articulate the things they have experienced; and giving thanks helps them interpret them in a positive way, enhancing their overall happiness.

Our children are precious gifts

I keep coming back to the idea of enjoying our children just because they are the most amazing, precious gifts. We know as parents that our children are the most important things in our lives. Sometimes we get wrapped up with the mundane things that might be happening in life; sometimes we have hang-ups about what we have not done, feel guilty and judge ourselves; or we beat ourselves up about the things that we feel we are doing badly, and compare ourselves to other parents.

I used to ask myself, "Why is everyone parenting better than me?" "What am I doing wrong?" These questions stopped me from being who I needed to be for my children. If you do this, too, I encourage you to think about reframing those disempowering questions, as I did.

Once I started to ask more empowering questions it helped me to see things from a positive perspective. I recommend asking questions such as:

"What am I doing well as a parent?"

"What are my strengths that I can pass on to my children?"

"What am I learning from being a parent?"

"What can I do to be a better parent than I was yesterday?"

"What are my children teaching me?"

"How can I love my children more?"

"What do my children need?"

These empowering questions help parenting become easier. I no longer raise my voice – something I used to do when my children were younger. Even with my training and experience I was totally overwhelmed, felt that I was not doing the job properly, felt I knew nothing about parenting.

Being able to take stock, look at the positive side and articulate, "I can choose how I feel about this situation" is really empowering. We can choose to feel overwhelmed or we can choose to feel good about being a parent and enjoy the experience.

Using affirmations

Affirmations help to focus the mind. Mine was, "My children are my greatest teachers." This turned challenges into enjoyable experiences. Find your own mantra or affirmation, which is authentic to you.

It could come back to your chosen parenting metaphor: "Parenting is a gift", "Parenting is a joy". Whatever you choose, it gives a focus which impacts on everything you say and do with your children. Choose well, and it will help you have a wonderful relationship with them.

A calm, connected and conscious life

I used to be afraid of those moments of doubt, frustration and big emotions of guilt. For me, the answer was to feel it and then choose to do something about it. The key to that was to acknowledge the connection between feelings and actions.

We have the ability to change the feeling of fear, in the fight-or-flight moment, to one of being calm and truly connected with our children with compassion and empathy. Only then can we be really conscious about what we say and what we do with our children. If we can do that, we are living and modelling a calm, connected and conscious life, and giving an amazing gift to our children.

We are showing our children that there is a positive way of dealing with any situation or challenge. We are showing up as being the best that we can be. As a result, our children will be empathetic, compassionate, optimistic and ultimately happy, being the best that they can be, too.

Reflection

*"Every time we remember to say "thank you",
we experience nothing less than heaven on
earth."*

Sarah Ban Breathnach

Activity

*Practice the Enjoy, Learn, Thanks (ELT) exercise with
your children.*

*Have a daily practice of deep, conscious breathing,
even if it is for just a couple of minutes a day. Think
of it like the need to clean your teeth for two minutes
a day, and it then becomes a habit.*

Give yourself an "enjoyment" of parenting rating from 1 to 10 (with 10 being the best it could be)

My current enjoyment rating _____

What would raising the rating by just one look like? What would your partner, children, friend notice if you were one more?

Give yourself a living in the "now" rating from 1 to 10 (with 10 being the best it could be)

My current "now" rating _____

What would raising the rating by just one look like? What would your partner, children, friend notice if you were one more?

Give yourself a gratitude "thanks" rating from 1 to 10 (with 10 being the best it could be)

My current gratitude rating _____

What would raising the rating by just one look like? What would your partner, children, friend notice if you were one more?

TO MY BOYS – "THANK YOU"

Thank you for crying because it has taught me to feel emotions more openly.

Thank you for your anger as it has helped me realise I need to love more.

Thank you for saying, "I don't care" as it has helped me to show compassion.

Thank you for asking me "why?" as that has helped me to question more.

Thank you for being frustrated because it has taught me to ask you what you need.

Thank you for not listening to me. I have learned to connect more.

Thank you for getting excited, as it has taught me how to live in the moment.

Thank you for the arguments as it has showed me how to be calm.

Thank you for saying "no" as it has taught me to say "yes" to life.

Thank you for not saying "thank you." It has shown me that when you do say it, you really feel it.

Thank you for your honesty because it has helped me to feel gratitude.

Thank you for being my greatest teachers and for being you.

Love, joy and peace.

Linda

~~~~~~~~~~~~~~~

ABOUT THE AUTHOR

Dr Linda Mallory is a parent and educational psychologist who has worked with hundreds of parents, teachers and children over the last twenty-five years.

Linda taught in Primary Schools as a class teacher, Reading Recovery Teacher and Special Needs Co-ordinator before becoming an Educational Psychologist.

Linda is a parent coach working with individuals and groups, helping parents develop a deeper connection, to have an amazing relationship with their children.

Linda lives in Bath with her husband, Av, and two boys, Fred and Tom, along with the family cat Yoda.

Thank you for reading

Parentuality

I would love to connect with you on your parenting journey. Receive regular positive parenting insights by signing up to useful resources and newsletter on The Why Parent website www.thewhyparent.com.

Email me at dr.lindamallory@thewhyparent.com

Find me on Facebook: "The Why Parent"

Contact me on LinkedIn: Dr Linda Mallory or Twitter: @thewhyparent

I welcome your feedback.

Please post your review on Amazon

With love and gratitude,

Linda.